Beginning
the
Principalship

WITHDRAWN

A publication jointly sponsored by

National Association of Elementary School Principals

National Association of Secondary School Principals

Beginning
the
Principalship

A Practical Guide for New School Leaders

John C. Daresh
Marsha A. Playko

CORWIN PRESS, INC.
A Sage Publications Company
Thousand Oaks, California

For information address:

Corwin Press, Inc.
A Sage Publications Company
2455 Teller Road
Thousand Oaks, California 91320
e-mail: order@corwin.sagepub.com

SAGE Publications Ltd.
6 Bonhill Street
London EC2A 4PU
United Kingdom

SAGE Publications India Pvt. Ltd.
M-32 Market
Greater Kailash I
New Delhi 110 048 India

Printed in the United States of America

Library of Congress Cataloging-in-Publication Data

Daresh, John C.
    Beginning the principalship : a practical guide for new school leaders / authors, John C. Daresh, Marsha A. Playko.
        p.   cm.
    Includes bibliographical references.
    ISBN 0-8039-6567-2 (pbk. : acid-free paper). — ISBN 0-8039-6566-4 (cloth : acid-free paper)
    1. School principals—United States.   2. School management and organization—United States.   3. Educational leadership—United States.   I. Playko, Marsha A., 1950-1996.   II. Title.
    LB2831.92.D37   1997
    371.2'012'0973—dc21   96-51287

This book is printed on acid-free paper.

    98 99 00 01 10 9 8 7 6 5 4 3 2

Corwin Press Production Editor: S. Marlene Head
Editorial Assistant: Nicole Fountain
Typesetter: Rebecca Evans
Cover Designer: Marcia R. Finlayson

Contents

Acknowledgments

A FEW WEEKS before the completion of this book, Marsha Playko lost her battle with cancer. She died on August 22, 1996. As her illness progressed during the last year, we had the opportunity to work on this project, share ideas, argue about specific items, and return to our beginning commitment to providing a resource to our colleagues who are now beginning their careers as school principals. As a result, this book is dedicated to Marsha, and it is important that the first acknowledgment is to her many contributions over the past few years of preparing this work. So much of Marsha was devoted to children, schools, teachers, and improving education. She loved being a principal, and so many tips and suggestions found in these pages came from her constant efforts to share that love with others who want to walk that same path.

We also acknowledge our good friend and supporter, Lloyd Chilton, formerly of Macmillan and Scholastic, who encouraged us to begin this project and remained our ally over the years.

We also have valued Gracia Alkema of Corwin Press as she stepped in to work with us during the final stages of manuscript preparation and development by a company so clearly committed to helping educational leaders achieve their goals.

Many others have also been helpful to this work. Ron Areglado of the National Association of Elementary School Principals showed continuing concern for our work, as did his colleague Gail Donovan. John Morefield of the Seattle Public Schools and John Lammel of the National Association of Secondary School Principals gave us encouragement in our efforts, and Don Gainey of the Milford, Massachusetts schools read earlier drafts and provided us with numerous important insights. We also heard from our friend, Scott Thomson of the National Policy Board for Educational Administration, as well as reviewers recruited by Corwin Press. We appreciated the input from so many friends.

Finally, we thank our families for again providing us with the understanding and time to work on another writing project—for one last time.

JOHN C. DARESH
MARSHA A. PLAYKO

About the Authors

John C. Daresh currently serves as the Chair of the Department of Educational Leadership and Foundations at the University of Texas at El Paso, where he also directs the university's new doctoral program in Educational Leadership. Prior to coming to Texas, he worked at Illinois State University, the University of Cincinnati, The Ohio State University (where he also directed that institution's Danforth Foundation Principal Preparation Program), and the University of Northern Colorado. He has worked as a consultant and speaker for school districts, universities, and state departments of education across the United States and in numerous countries around the world. Most recently, he served as a member of the NASSP/Carnegie Commission to Restructure the American High School and the National Association of Elementary School Principals (NAESP), and he continues to work with NAESP in a variety of professional development activities to serve its members.

Daresh began his career by working in the public schools of Dubuque, Iowa, and Chicago. He received his doctorate from the University of Wisconsin–Madison.

Marsha A. Playko served for 5 years as the principal of Hazelwood Elementary School in Newark, Ohio, prior to her death in the summer of 1996. During that time, she also worked as a consultant to numerous agencies across the United States and abroad. She also worked as the Associate Director of the LEAD Project for the state of Ohio and with John Daresh as the Project Administrator for the Danforth Foundation Principal Preparation Program at The Ohio State University, the institution from which she earned both her master's and doctoral degrees. She began her career as an educator by serving for several years as an elementary school teacher in the Groveport, Ohio schools. During the past few years, Playko became involved as a member of the task force convened by NAESP to review its work, *Proficiencies for Principals*.

Playko is survived by her husband, Richard, also a school administrator, and her three children, Kelly, Nick, and Mark. Her passing leaves a significant void in the field of administrator professional development.

Introduction

THIS BOOK ADDRESSES a paradox in American education. On one hand, research that has been directed toward identifying the reasons why some schools are more effective than others has shown repeatedly that of all the variables that may have something to do with making some schools more successful, one stands out. That most critical variable is the leadership behavior of the school principal. Good schools have good principals. On the other hand, the role of the school principal is becoming more complex and difficult each day. Greater pressures are being placed on principals today.

Added to this mix of realities is the fact that more inexperienced school principals are taking their first administrative assignments each year. However, despite the importance of the principalship and the difficulties attached to that job, few efforts are being made to help newcomers succeed. In a few cases, individual states have enacted policies requiring induction support to be provided to beginners, although those policies are not reinforced with sufficient funding to enable people to receive much ongoing support. The fact is that in many cases, new principals are still facing entry into school systems where a prevailing message from other principals is, "You'll just have to learn the ropes like I did—through trial and error." Even more remarkable is the tone set in other settings, exemplified by the comment of one experienced superintendent who once told us, "When I hire a new principal, I expect that person to take charge and run his or her school. I don't have time to provide a lot of 'hand-holding.' "

We are not arguing in this book that service to one's personal survival as a rookie principal should ever be viewed as more important than effective service to students. But we are suggesting that when a person is handed the keys to a multi-million-dollar facility, and is also given responsibility for overseeing the quality of life for hundreds (or thousands) of children and dozens (or hundreds) of adults, it only makes sense that every effort be made to provide help and assistance on a regular basis.

Through the chapters of this book, we offer some insights into how you, as a new school principal, might be able to find some ways to "walk the tightrope" between surviving your first years on the job and also beginning to serve as a strong and effective instructional leader. As you review each chapter, we invite you to begin to develop a personal portfolio or action plan to guide your work. Many questions are asked throughout the book as a way to help you focus on your planning process.

In the long run, nothing will guarantee your success as an effective principal. Books such as this one, networks, mentoring relationships, and participation in activities sponsored by professional associations may help, but they will not be sufficient without your hard work and personal commitment to take the first steps toward becoming a successful school leader. But we hope that you will never feel alone or without a great deal of support as you begin your journey.

1

Why This Book Is Important

David Griswald: A Typical Rookie

DAVID GRISWALD was an elementary school teacher for about 10 years when he decided that he wanted more out of his professional life than what he saw from his third-grade classroom. He loved working with children, but he long ago realized that he could not spend the rest of his life without some further challenges and opportunities for career advancement. As a result, he began taking graduate courses in educational administration at nearby Heathrow University, with the hope that he would soon qualify for and become an elementary school principal.

David's dream became reality last spring. He had completed all the courses needed to receive his principal's certificate at the end of the previous winter term, and a few months later, he applied for the principalship at Spirit Lake Elementary School, the smallest and oldest building in the Green Valley Schools. It is now October, nearly 4 months after David was named principal, and 7 weeks after his first school year began. David continues to be glad about his choice of seeking a principalship, but there are times when the excitement and enthusiasm he felt back in June and July begin to fade. At times, David wonders if he wouldn't really rather return to the good old days in his third-grade classroom.

The single most frustrating thing that David feels is not that he can't handle the job of managing his school. He has a good secretary and a very experienced and talented teaching staff, and he feels as if he got some very practical things out of the internship he completed last year as part of his Heathrow training. What he is concerned about is the kind of emotional drain that this new way of life is causing him. He knew there would be conflict as an administrator—after all, there is an old saying that "Administrators aren't paid to win popularity contests." Further, he is truly surprised at the number of personnel issues he has to deal with each day. On top of that, he suddenly recognizes how lonely he is beginning to feel in his office. Dr. Pringle, the superintendent of schools, was very supportive when he handed David the keys to his building last summer, but now he rarely comes by to visit, encourage David, or even ask how things are going. The other seven elementary school principals in the district are friendly enough; they invite David to play golf with them every once in a while. But they are also extremely busy with their work at school. And they never want to "talk shop" when they get together.

All of this makes David Griswald feel very much like a real rookie who has no connection with anyone or anything.

*   *   *

National surveys conducted by the National Association of Elementary School Principals (NAESP) and the National Association of Secondary School Principals (NASSP) have consistently shown that within the next few years, more than half the principals in the United States (and in many other countries around the world) will be able to retire and leave the school principalship if they so desire. Also, there are many areas in this country where there is a steady growth in population. As a result of these factors, more and more people will be going into school principalships for the first time.

At the same time that we will see more and more "rookie" principals, however, it must be recognized that society is changing rapidly. As a result, students in schools are changing drastically, and the business of running schools is changing as well. The principalship has never been an easy job. The last several years have made the job even more difficult and demanding.

Based on your experience as a teacher, list some of the ways in which changes that you have seen in the nature of your community, school district, or students have drastically changed your role as a professional educator. (For example, increases in single-parent families have undoubtedly changed the nature of some of the parental support you may have expected just a few years ago. Perhaps there have been many new students for whom English is not their primary language moving into your school district.)

_____

_____

_____

_____

If you are not currently a school principal, you can imagine how the issues raised in your list above have made the life of school principals today different from what was seen only a few years ago. If you are a principal, you probably already know that these issues have a significant effect on your work each day.

The effect that all of these changes have had on the work of school principals is profound. As a consequence, traditional patterns of accommodating newcomers to principalships are less acceptable. In the past, it was possible for the superintendent to hand the school keys to the new principal and simply advise, "You're the boss now. Try not to foul things up too badly this first year. Learn on the job from those with more experience." Such haphazard approaches to supporting educational leaders first coming on board are not consistent with the increased expectations and demands by parents and other community members that schools become more productive and effective places. Simply stated, there is less "wiggle room" for new principals than ever before. Rookies must now step aboard and perform with the same skill and effectiveness as colleagues who have been in leadership positions for many years. The beginning principal today often faces a work environment where little or no tolerance is seen for those who might make mistakes. State and federal mandates define much of what principals are supposed to do, whereas central offices and local school board members are less tolerant of errors and poor performance than ever before. And, because all school administrators now face these same pressures for "perfect" performance, beginning principals are not always able to find supportive relationships with their more experienced colleagues.

In this book, we are not going to pretend that we will offer some magic recipes that can be followed by beginning principals such as our case study, David Griswald. We are not going to give you a simple list of 10 or 11 ideas and practices that will always lead you to success. However, we are going to share some insights that have been derived from our experiences, and also from research conducted over the years related to the needs of beginning school principals. We have learned quite a bit about the kinds of things that might help David Griswald and you as you proceed through the opening stages of your administrative career in schools. One of the most important things that we have discovered is that from the start of your life as a school leader, you can always look at your new job in two very different, often competing, ways:

- How to survive the principalship
- How to be an educational leader

These two ideas are certainly not mutually exclusive. As many school administrators point out, you cannot become a leader of schools if you do not survive your first few days in the principalship. But there are many individuals who look to the challenge of the principalship only in terms of "making it through" from one day to the next. They tend to think only in terms of short-term skills—how to stay out of trouble, or how not to get fired.

In the chapters that follow, we will share with you some of the kinds of things that will help to keep you from losing your job, to be certain. However, we caution you that simple survivorship will only be a small part of what we will describe. The legacy that we wish to share with you is one of leadership development—how even the "greenest rookie" can position himself or herself so that more effective school practice will result. If we did not take this stance, we would not be doing what we believe is supportive of the best practices of school principals. After all, we believe that effective principals will lead effective schools and that effective schools are what we all try to develop and maintain.

Plan for the Book

We will proceed through this book with a review of many of the issues and concerns often faced by beginning principals. These concerns are described through a conceptual framework that we develop and explain in Chapter 2. Included will be not only a statement of some of the problems frequently faced by beginners but also some strategies that you might wish to follow in dealing with these problems.

Later chapters will explore other aspects of life as a new school principal. In each chapter, we will look at one or more of the major issues faced by beginning principals. For example, Chapter 3 discusses the value of developing a clear educational platform, or statement of professional values, to guide your work. This is one method of helping you to develop greater self-awareness regarding your abilities as you assume your new professional role.

An important part of each chapter will be a concluding section where we ask you to develop a personal plan for improvement and professional development that is consistent with the issues discussed in that chapter. Through this technique, we believe that we will assist you in the creation of a professional portfolio and personal growth plan that may help you reflect on your first years as a principal. More and more school systems and even states are demanding that administrative personnel create portfolios as a way to guide their personal and professional development. Although we agree that such practices can be very useful ways to assist educators become more focused on their career needs, we see that in many cases, portfolios are little more than scrapbooks that include a lot of random, disconnected artifacts. Through the responses that you will be able to provide in the personal plan sections throughout this book, we hope that your portfolio can become a way to lead you through the next important steps in your career.

Suggested Readings

A few additional books that you may wish to consult regarding issues often faced by first-time principals and other managers of different organizations include the following:

Belker, L. B. (1993). *The first-time manager* (3rd ed.). New York: American Management Association.

Car, C. (1989). *The new manager's survival guide*. New York: Wiley.

Champion, A. N. (1992). *The new supervisor*. Los Altos, CA: Crisp.

Daresh, J. C., & Playko, M. A. (1989). *A resource guide for the Ohio Entry Year Standard*. Westerville, OH: The Ohio LEAD Project.

Hill, L. A. (1992). *Becoming a manager: How new managers master the challenges of leadership*. New York: Penguin.

2

A Framework for Understanding the Beginning Principalship

FEWER THAN 10 YEARS AGO, concerns of beginning principals were not really considered important by educational researchers. The truth of that statement is readily apparent if you take time to glance at the literature in educational administration over the past 50 years. There are many books and articles that are focused on the role of the principal, of course. We know a lot about the duties of principals, the kinds of conceptual and practical skills that must be demonstrated, and we even have excellent descriptions of what the life of a school principal is like. For example, Harry Wolcott's (1969) classic study, *The Man in the Principal's Office*, is still viewed by many as the best analysis of what building administrators do on a daily basis.

Because of the recognition that there is a critical need for new people to move into principalships across the nation, however, there has been an equivalent understanding that research related to the world of novice administrators would not only be interesting but important as a way to inform the development of policies and practices. In this chapter, we will look at some of the most recent analyses of beginning principals' work and use it to form a way that you might compare the kinds of issues that you face with what other principals have said and experienced when they first "came on board."

As a way to review some of the research findings, let us consider three brief cases of first-year principals. Each case is based on research data obtained when we asked beginners what some of their frustrations have been in the first year on the job.

Case Study: Figuring Out the Papers

Mary Auburn was in the first 2 weeks of her first principalship of an elementary school. She had waited for nearly 3 years after completing required university courses to qualify for a state administrative certificate before she actually applied for a position. This was due in large measure to the fact that her youngest child was still not in elementary school, and Mary felt it unwise to take on the responsibilities of the principalship with a young child still at home.

Like many beginning principals, Mary got word that she had landed her first administrative post during the summer. It was actually mid-July before she received final, official approval of her appointment from the school board of the Apple Junction Schools. She had attended the board meeting where she was introduced as the new principal at Big Fjord Primary, a small but well-respected school in the district. The next day, Mary proudly went to the central office to get her keys, policy manual, and all other assorted paraphernalia, mail, and notes left from the previous principal. She began to skim over the mound of paper in front of her and suddenly she began to get quite uneasy about her new job. She knew that a big part of her work as a school principal would involve keeping records and filling out forms, but she now was nearly overwhelmed by how to fill out district forms, complete state department of education report sheets, and respond to the memos, correspondence, and all of the other paperwork that filled her in-basket. She had a lot of similar paper to deal with when she was teacher, but that experience was minimal compared to what she was now experiencing as a regular part of her administrative world.

Case Study: Am I Supposed to Go?

Dan Carter was very happy to become an elementary principal in the Hightower Independent Schools. He had dreamed of stepping in as a principal for the past 2 years while he completed courses leading to administrative certification. The night when the board of education approved his appointment was a great time for Dan and his family. Everyone came to the board meeting in June, and then there was a nice reception for Dan and the three other new principals in the district. Dan noted that the other elementary school principals attended the board meeting, so he penciled in the first and third Tuesday of every month as an evening when he would be away from home, sitting in on school board meetings.

In July, Dan came to both school board meetings. He wasn't terribly surprised to note that he was the only principal in attendance. After all, his more experienced colleagues were probably on vacation. Veterans deserved to miss the ceremonies every once in a while, and as a rookie, he had a right to be "gung ho" this first month.

When August came around, and all the principals in the district were due back in town for the next school year, Dan again went to both school board meetings. Again, however, he noted that he was the only building principal in attendance. He expected some recognition from the superintendent, and he hoped that he would be getting some "brownie points" by showing up for board meetings. However, there was not even a hint that the superintendent saw him in the middle of the board room. Dan had now spent about 14 hours over the past 2 months attending school board meetings, none of which had even the slightest relevance to his role as a school principal in the district.

Enough was enough. In September, Dan decided that staying home with his family was worth much more than he was likely to get in terms of central office administrators' appreciation as a "good company man" by attending yet another board meeting. However, on the first Wednesday in September, when the district principals had their monthly gathering with the assistant superintendent for administrative services, Dan was the subject of considerable derision from his colleagues. "Hey, rookie, you didn't make it to the board meeting last night," noted Rob Gretzky, one of the more experienced principals in the district. "The superintendent scanned the room and noticed the principals who were there. You won't hear anything directly, but the superintendent has a long memory."

Dan felt bad, but he knew that this was the first board meeting of the new school year, so he assumed that he would now be expected to attend board meetings every 2 weeks. In the third week of September, however, he again appeared at the board meeting, but he discovered that he was the only building administrator present. The superintendent only stared blankly at him.

"What the heck am I supposed to do with these board meetings?" Dan asked Mary Sheehan, another elementary principal who had been in the district for more than 10 years. "I show up and I am the only principal there, so the boss gets mad. I don't show up, and I hear that the boss gets mad. Am I being set up here for a big fall here, or what?"

Mary smiled at Dan's frustration. "You've got to be able to read the signs from the coach's box, Dan. When the superintendent wants us to show up at board meetings, there are signs. When the board has anything to do with curriculum, student discipline, or any community social events, you'd better be there. Otherwise, the boss wants to be the show himself. Read your advanced board meeting agenda very carefully the next Friday before a board meeting!"

The revelation as to what the "signals" were hit Dan like a ton of bricks. From that point on, he figured out the system and didn't miss an important board meeting.

Case Study: I'm No Politician

Karen Carlisle had been waiting for the past 2 years for the day when she could take her first principalship. Despite many difficulties and conflicts in her personal life, she persisted in her efforts to complete a program of studies leading to certification at a local university. She interviewed with several school districts before getting her first big chance to take over a principalship of a small but well-regarded elementary school in a community near her home. Like many individuals, she found out that she was to be a new principal only a few weeks before the next school year was to start. Still, she was on "Cloud Nine" as August wore on and she got ready for the arrival of her teachers, classified staff, and most importantly, her students.

One of the things that Karen was looking forward to in her first principalship was the ability to work effectively with her teachers on a daily basis. For years as a classroom teacher, she was concerned with the fact that principals seemed to be getting farther away from their instructional duties more each year. Karen saw this first job as an opening for her to get into a school and truly become an instructional leader. She would devote her time to working with students, teachers, staff, and parents of the students in her school. Not only was this a personal goal, but it seemed to be an idea that was strongly supported by the school district and superintendent. When she stated that her goal was to "take first things first" in her school by working with the people in her immediate community, the interviewing team and superintendent all made comments about how that was exactly the attitude they wanted to see in a new principal.

Things appeared to be going very well for Karen in her first few weeks as a principal. However, about a month into the school year, she received a call from Dr. Don Adams, who explained that he was the president of a local community organization that had been formed to ensure that schools would be sensitive to the needs of the businesses in town. It was a very pleasant conversation, and Karen explained to Dr. Adams that she appreciated his call but that for the moment, she could not become actively involved with a lot of organizations in the community that did not work directly with her students, parents, and teachers. After all, she was the principal of a small elementary school where few parents were directly involved with the local Chamber of Commerce. Karen thought to herself that the group headed by Dr. Adams had very little apparent direct connection with her world and that her time was better spent keeping to her original goals.

As the year progressed, however, Karen began to receive a number of subtle signs from the central office and parents in her own school to the effect that Dr. Adams's group was not pleased by being turned away from her school. Karen began to understand that what seemed to be a task not connected to her world as a building principal was beginning to have more and more of a negative effect on her daily life as a school administrator.

* * *

These three brief scenarios have been deliberately selected from our files to illustrate three "classic" situations representing the kinds of issues faced by many "rookie" school principals. In the first case, Mary Auburn is a beginning principal who is faced with the enormous demands of her new job; papers fill her desk, her superintendent wants answers to every question "right now," and the district policy manual seems to be staring at Mary in a way that suggests that she had better know every intricate detail of the manual before she dares to do anything, or else she will be perceived as an incompetent rookie.

Research related to the needs and concerns of beginning principals has shown that Mary's concerns are common issues. Often, these are referred to as the "technical side" or "managerial side" of the principalship. These involve the operational details associated with providing direction and order for a school. Some might even say that these skills are needed to "keep the trains running—on time." Included may be such things as how to make certain that the policies of the district are followed and that there is compliance with state rules and regulations. It involves keeping things in line with the formal duties and job descriptions of principals. The technical side of the principalship also involves properly overseeing and maintaining accounts and the school budget, maintaining effective relations with parents and others in the community, developing a weekly schedule of important events and activities, delegating responsibilities to others, keeping student discipline and a safe and orderly physical environment in the school, resolving disputes, and ensuring that all terms of the district's master contract or negotiated agreement with the teachers' association are always addressed. All of these technical and managerial issues are often referred to as the "beans, buses, and budgets" dimension of school administration.

It would be incorrect to leave this discussion of important technical demands of the job without noting that for many beginning principals, a major stumbling block is not solely the inability to do certain managerial tasks associated with their jobs. In fact, they might be quite skilled at doing some of the things required in their job descriptions. Rather, many beginners have significant problems because they lack strong communication skills. In short, they know what to do, but they cannot communicate to others *why* they must do what they do. That lack of communication involves both written and oral expression skills. The critical issue here is that even the best administrative "technician" with the best ideas and motives for managing the school can fail if others do not understand what is taking place.

What are some of the technical and managerial aspects of your job as a school principal that concern you in the early stage of your career? (For example, have you discovered that you are not terribly confident about budgeting or the use of technology as part of your daily job requirements?)

_____

_____

_____

_____

_____

_____

The second case study, in which Dan Carter had a hard time understanding when he should or should not attend school board meetings, is also representative of problems often reported by novice school principals. In short, the research refers to these as "problems with socialization." These types of concerns are often related to two different points: socialization to the norms and culture within a particular school district, and also socialization to the profession of educational administration in general.

Dan Carter was experiencing frustration in his new job because he could not figure out how to read the subtle signs of "what's going on" in his new environment. It made sense to him to attend school board meetings, but he could not understand why he was discouraged from being present in some cases, whereas at other times, he seemed to be in trouble when absent. There was no rational pattern that could be followed. What Dave did not appreciate was some of the background history that other principals in the district knew.

Not knowing about the culture, traditions, and history of schools and school districts often hinders new principals in their ability to do their jobs. This gets played out in a variety of different ways. Informal "dress codes," participation in administration social events (e.g., holiday parties, golf outings, etc.), or even how to address the superintendent's secretary (e.g., never use a first name, or always use a first name) are all examples of the "little things" that need to be understood by a newcomer.

List other examples of some of the local traditions, cultures, or past practices that you have discovered as part of your new setting. (For example, perhaps you have discovered that there is a tradition in your school where Fridays are "dress down" days for the staff or that teachers do not "talk business" at the table during lunch periods.)

_____

_____

_____

_____

_____

The second type of socialization problems often faced by new principals is found in learning about the culture of the principalship as a career. Here we are talking about trying to understand the "big picture" of how principals are supposed to act, what they are supposed to know, and even what they are supposed to do, when compared with colleagues around the nation. Perhaps the best way to summarize this area is through the question, "So, what does a principal look like?"

Many new principals become so focused on surviving their first years on the job that they ignore the importance of learning what is going on in the professional world outside of their own vision. They are unaware of critical issues that are facing colleagues in other parts of their own states and across the nation. In recent years, it has been amazing to see the number of principals who were "blindsided" by issues that were faced by principals in other parts of the country. An example might be the ways in which community pressure groups have focused on such apparently harmless curricular innovations as "outcomes-based education" and made these practices the center of considerable controversy. It is understandable that local principals feel as if they must tend to local issues first. However, at the same time, there are national trends that are under way that will eventually affect the local scene. The fact that beginning principals are not being socialized to the larger profession often makes this kind of continuing communication with the "outside world" into a serious problem.

In the space below, jot down a few additional items that you have discovered to be issues that are faced by other principals across the nation and that you have discovered in issues that you must also face in your first few years on the job. (For example, has the issue of allowing prayers in school been something that you have had to address in your school or district? What about the arrival of large groups of students for whom English is not their native language?)

The third case was that of Karen Carlisle, the new principal who was surprised to discover that her work as an elementary principal would also need to include some time as a link with important groups out in the community. She could not maintain her personal image of a principal being involved only with business within the walls of her school. Although it may not have been part of her personal vision of the principalship, she was learning that there are certain political responsibilities that "come with the turf."

Researchers have found this theme to be present in many beginning principals. Often, this is referred to as becoming effectively socialized to a new role, or having an awareness of self. Other examples occur when new principals are faced with critical decisions that might be very different from their own sense of personal values or even ethics. An example of this might be when a beginner is faced with the responsibility of evaluating a teacher and knows that the evaluative process may end in the nonrenewal or even termination of that individual's job. Is it really a part of one's own values and ability to carry out a process that may deprive a colleague of his or her career as a teacher? Another related issue might be situations where a new principal observes teachers who are not performing effectively but, upon reviewing personnel files, finds nothing but "excellent" or even "superior" ratings from the last principal. Are the perceptions of the new principal incorrect? Or have these teachers suddenly become ineffective during the last few months? Or was the previous principal too lenient or unable (or unwilling) to evaluate teachers effectively? Couple this issue with the need for a newcomer not to alienate experienced teachers too quickly, and another important conflict for a novice administrator appears.

All of these issues center around the image that a person has in his or her mind relative to being a principal. Later, in Chapter 8, we consider some other ways in which a beginning principal must appreciate his or her role of being a "boss." Here, we simply note that from many studies of beginning principals, it is clear that people often suffer a kind of shock when their personal value system is threatened by the kinds of things that they are called upon by others to do. Can you think of any examples of how your personal awareness of what you must do as a principal has been different from what you expected of that role?

Balance Is the Key

In the preceding sections, we described some of the kinds of problem areas identified by many researchers in the professional lives of beginning principals. A review of these broad areas—technical skills, socialization, and self-awareness or role awareness—often leads a person to try to understand and generalize along the lines of deciding which area is most important if one is to succeed in the principalship. One of the things that we want to emphasize here is that research on beginning principals has shown consistently that *all three* areas are important. In some ways, that fact makes your job even harder. It is not possible to simply "take care of business" by doing nothing more than addressing technical skills for the first year or two, for example. This type of logic often is heard among novices who state that they want to get established as good managers first, with the assumption that they can take care of other matters (e.g., socialization and self-awareness or role awareness) at some time in the future.

Our research related to the critical skills that should be demonstrated by successful beginning principals has looked at the issue of how to address the three areas of concern identified earlier. We asked different groups of educational administrators to indicate their perceptions of the relative importance of certain job tasks that were, in turn, classified as belonging to the groupings of technical skills, socialization skills, or self-awareness skills. When we asked principals with at

least 5 years of experience to rate the importance of individual tasks for success
and "survival" by beginning colleagues, we discovered that they ranked the three
critical skill areas in the following way.

1. Socialization skills (most important)
2. Self-awareness and role awareness skills
3. Technical and managerial skills (least important)

When we asked superintendents who had recently (i.e., within the past 3
years) hired at least one new principal for their districts, we discovered the following ranking.

1. Self-awareness and role awareness skills
2. Socialization skills
3. Technical and managerial skills

Finally, we found that those who were enrolled in university programs leading to certification or licensure ranked these three areas as follows.

1. Technical and managerial skills
2. Socialization skills
3. Self-awareness and role awareness skills

These findings suggest a few very important things about the nature of issues
faced by beginning principals. First, there are clearly some important differences
in the rankings. Those who have little or no experience as school principals rate
technical skills as the most critical issue that needs to be addressed in order to be
successful. However, as people are more experienced as administrators, they may
downgrade the importance of carrying out technical skills and identify socialization and self-awareness (coupled with appreciating the expectations of others) as
being more critical to effectiveness. Or they develop skills in delegating some technical duties to others, even though there is a recognition that the technical side of
the job is important, but not necessarily that it must consume the complete interests of the principal all the time.

The second thing that we point out, however, is that whatever the differences
may be when comparing one group's perceptions with another, no group indicates
that any of the three skill areas is unimportant. In other words, we might suggest
that experienced administrators do not indicate that technical and managerial
skills are as important as the other areas. However, this group still includes as
important the performance of technical aspects of the principalship. Socialization

and self-awareness are more important, but no one should assume that daily managerial duties should not be carried out.

The key to effectiveness and survival, we believe, is the development of a proper balance among the three critical skill areas. The management of the school (i.e., technical and managerial skills) must be done along with attention to "fitting in" (i.e., socialization) and the demonstration of knowing what the job is all about and how it affects the individual person (self-awareness or role awareness).

Suggestions for Improvement and Professional Development

Some suggestions for activities that you might carry out to assist in your professional development related to the three critical skill areas in our framework include the following.

Technical and Managerial Skills

- Seek an experienced principal in your district to serve as a "job coach" who can share some "tricks of the trade" related to some of the technical and managerial parts of doing your job more effectively.

- Consider participating in a leadership assessment program such as the Administrator Diagnostic Inventory developed by the National Association of Elementary School Principals (NAESP) This activity will provide insights to you about your personal strengths and areas needing further development in leadership and management skills.

- Make an agreement with one or more of the experienced principals in your district to allow you to visit their schools and shadow them as they engage in the daily management tasks associated with their jobs.

- If you are lucky enough to find an experienced secretary outside your door, or if you find teachers with whom you have rapport, ask them for their insights into the kinds of managerial or technical issues that merit special attention in your school.

- Review some of the practical tips suggested in Chapter 6.

- Identify short-term workshops or seminars related to more effective performance of the technical aspects of the job that might be sponsored by local, state, or national professional associations.

Socialization

- Work with your job coach and ask questions about the traditions, past practices, and general culture of your school.

- Read carefully a random selection of past school board agendas and minutes to determine if there appear to be patterns of practices that you need to learn more about.

- Go out of your way to attend lunches, breakfasts, and other social events that might enable you to gain greater insights into some of the issues that are shared concerns of your colleagues.

- Spend time getting to know the personality and characteristics of the community within your school—get to know students, staff, and your teachers as people, not simply as those people who happen to come into "your" school each day. After all, the faster that it becomes "our" school, the better.

- Listen and watch in the ways described in greater detail in Chapter 9 of this book.

- Become an active participant in activities and events sponsored by professional associations of school administrators. Read such publications as the National Association of Secondary School Principals' *Bulletin* and *Principal*, published by the National Association of Elementary School Principals.

Self-Awareness and Role Awareness Skills

- Identify a personal mentor either within your school district or within some other school system to help you in getting feedback about your career development. This person may or may not be the same person selected as a job coach to help you learn more about technical skills.

- Write and then periodically review your statement of personal professional values, or educational platform. For further information about this activity, review Chapter 3.

- Work with a trusted colleague who will agree to observe your work for a period of time and ask you to describe what you believe you were doing on the job. Compare and contrast your perceptions with those of someone looking at you "from the outside in."

Building a Personal Plan

In the spaces provided in the next few pages, we suggest that you begin the process of developing a personal professional growth plan, or portfolio, by reflecting on the key concepts described in this chapter and specifying some important personal goals that you might have related to each major issue. For each goal or set of goals, we believe that you need to identify activities that will assist you in achieving these goals. Also, you should note the ways in which you can assess your progress toward these goals and objectives.

Area I: Technical and Managerial Skill Development

Personal objectives related to this skill area for the next year:

_____

_____

_____

_____

_____

Some of the things that you will do to achieve these objectives:

_____

_____

_____

_____

_____

The ways in which someone will be able to tell if you have been successful in achieving your objectives are:

_____

_____

_____

_____

_____

Area 2: Socialization Skill Development

Personal objectives related to this skill area for the next year:

_____

_____

_____

_____

_____

_____

Some of the things that you will do to achieve these objectives:

_____

_____

_____

_____

_____

_____

The ways in which someone will be able to tell if you have been successful in achieving your objectives are:

_____

_____

_____

_____

_____

_____

_____

Area 3: Self-Awareness and Role Awareness Skills

Personal objectives related to this skill area for the next year:

_____

_____

_____

_____

_____

_____

Some of the things that you will do to achieve these objectives:

_____

_____

_____

_____

_____

_____

The ways in which someone will be able to tell if you have been successful in achieving your objectives are:

_____

_____

_____

_____

_____

_____

Reference

Wolcott, H. (1969). *The man in the principal's office*. New York: Holt, Rinehart & Winston.

3

Reviewing Personal Values

THERE ARE MANY REASONS why beginning principals experience difficulties during their first years on the job. In some cases, they do not "take care of business." For example, they might ignore the importance of completing assigned administrative tasks in a timely fashion, or they may violate local policies or even state laws. Another reason for people getting into trouble is that they do not seem to have the kinds of "people skills" needed to communicate effectively with parents, staff, other administrators, or even students.

In this chapter, however, we focus on yet another area that we have found to be a serious problem for many beginning school principals. Research related to beginning leadership problems tends to identify the importance of people coming to grips with their own set of personal values and priorities as they must engage in activities required of principals (Self-Awareness Skills, as identified in Chapter 2).

This chapter suggests a strategy that might be used as a way to identify important personal and professional values as a first step to walking into the principal's office for the first time.

Case Study: Because It's Important to Me

Charles Davis, principal at Thomas Jefferson High School, was in trouble. He had just gotten a call from Moira Kingsley, assistant superintendent for administrative services. She pointed out to Charles that for the 4th month in a row, he was at least 1 week late in turning in his Building Use Report Plan (BURP) to the central office. According to Moira, this was an important form because it provided a good deal of information regarding the ways in which Thomas Jefferson and all the other high schools in the district were being used by community groups in the evenings and on weekends. In turn, this information could be used in the superintendent's monthly report to the community to show how responsive the schools were to public needs and interests. And, with a bond election coming up in 6 months, it was critical for the district to "talk to the voters."

Charles offered his apologies, again, to Moira, and promised that he would get last month's report to her as soon as possible and that he would do his best to get this month's report to her on time. As soon as he hung up the phone, however, he looked at his calendar for the next 3 days and realized that it would be virtually impossible to find the time to fill in the report. The remainder of today was scheduled for classroom visitations. Charles had promised his teachers that he would be available to visit each teacher's classroom whenever the teacher felt he could be of assistance in that way. Further, Anne Marie Burkowitz, the assistant principal, had made a similar commitment to being "on call" for supervisory assistance. The secretaries in Charles's office were overloaded with tons of work resulting from the upcoming regional accreditation team visit. And both Charles and Anne Marie were going to be tied up the next 3 nights with different evening activities at the school. There was going to be a basketball game tonight against arch-rival Martin Luther King, a wrestling match tomorrow night, and a parent advisory community meeting on the next night. Tomorrow's schedule was also filled with classroom observations, and Charles also knew that a certain percentage of his time would be devoted to responding to whatever momentary problems walked into his office each day.

Charles knew within a minute after talking to Moira that he would be hearing from her again in a few days. But he also knew he was doing the best job he knew how to do, whether the central office recognized it or not.

* * *

School principals make hundreds of decisions every day. Each is made through certain lenses that the individual brings to the job. And the sources of these lenses are varied. Some come from written school board policy manuals. For example, a principal quickly decides that a secretary is entitled to take next Friday off to go to the doctor because the school district has a clear statement of what constitutes sick leave or personal leave. These are easy decisions to make in most cases. There are, however, other decisions that principals are called upon to make each day that are not easily defined, and which are not readily made according to the policy of the system.

Consider, for example, decisions such as the one that Charles Davis had to make in the case described above. Charles had to decide whether or not he would comply with the requirements of the school system and fill out his monthly report, or if he would use his time in other ways. What is the deciding factor? Charles's personal and professional values have a lot to do with his ultimate choice (and also the probable consequences resulting from his decisions). Charles Davis valued contact with his teachers and students more than he did a paper report form. No printed manual or other material guided his decision.

Most decisions made by principals are matters of personal choice. In many cases, it is unclear to the outside observer the reasons that principals use in making their decisions. Ms. Jones gets to take her class on a field trip, but Mr. Smith is not permitted to go. Bobby Wilson is given 3 days of in-school suspension, but Mary Pierce is simply reprimanded for the same offense and sent back to the classroom. Teachers complain about apparent inconsistencies in the visible behavior of the principal. Yet principals often do not seem concerned about what others believe are differential patterns of behavior. However, experienced principals have learned—often the hard way—that differences in perceptions, whether they are right or wrong, represent real beliefs and views of others. As a consequence, these perceptions must be understood, appreciated, and addressed.

In Chapter 2, we discussed the importance of developing a strong sense of self-awareness as a critical skill for beginning principals. In fact, we pointed out that of all the behaviors noted by superintendents, the most valued was the ability to show clearly one's personal beliefs and values, and a recognition of why one was selected for a leadership role in the first place. Incidentally, it will be interesting to see if this rating will be the same for Charles Davis's superintendent when he or she does not get the building report form once again!

Self-awareness about one's duties and responsibilities in a job comes about largely as the product of a reflective process in which one constantly matches the requirements of the job with a personal value system. The more a person is content that his or her choice of a career is consistent with the most important attitudes, beliefs, and values that drive that person, the happier he or she will be—and the more effective, productive, and ultimately, successful. It is a simple fact that when a person becomes more "invested" in a job as a personal commitment, he or she will be not only more satisfied but more effective as well.

The strategy that we suggest as a way to review one's personal value and belief systems as they may be related to the realities of the job of the principalship is through a periodic review of something called a personal educational platform. A platform is a philosophy statement, although we hesitate to call it by that name because we find that most practicing administrators avoid things that are too "philosophical" or "theoretical." A platform statement is a way to put into writing some of the "nearest and dearest" beliefs that a person might have relative to educational issues that define a major part of his or her work life. We often say that the "planks" in a platform express an individual's nonnegotiable values. In many ways, they represent core values of a person—the kinds of things that, if violated by the nature of the job one has to do or other factors, would cause that person to quit the job. A personal educational platform has the power of putting on paper the "bottom line" of an individual educator. Finally, a statement of a platform has the potential either to guide a person away from a professional role that is inconsistent with personal values or simply to enable a person to know when a particular placement in a job is not what was envisioned in the first place. For example, a platform can help a person recognize if selecting the principalship as a career goal was a good choice, or if taking a particular principalship in a specific community was the best move. In either case, if the personal values that are expressed in a platform are not attainable in a job in one location, it may be reasonable to move on.

Building a Platform

In the pages that follow, we will lead you through the development of an educational platform. There are many different approaches that might be followed in carrying out this exercise, and we invite you to modify anything that we offer here so that it is more consistent with your own needs, interests, and, of course, personal values.

We will ask several questions that have to do with central issues faced by educators, in most cases regardless of whether they work in classrooms or administrative offices. After each question, we provide space so that you might write your own responses. Simply "filling in the blanks" does not necessarily mean that you have prepared an educational platform. However, your answers below might serve as an important foundation for a more cohesive statement that will be crafted in the future.

1. What is my view of the purpose of schooling?

People have struggled with this issue for almost as long as there have been formal organizations called "schools." Is it your view that students attend these formal organizations in order to acquire vocational skills? For moral development? To develop "basic skills" primarily? To learn about good citizenship and other civic values? Perhaps there are other purposes that guide your vision, as noted in the space below.

_____

_____

_____

_____

_____

_____

2. What are the key ingredients of an "adequate" education for all students?

There is a lot of talk about how to get schools "back to basics." Although this phrase has become a kind of slogan for a particular conservative point of view regarding schooling, we believe that each educator must have some sense of what the basic elements of good schooling might include.

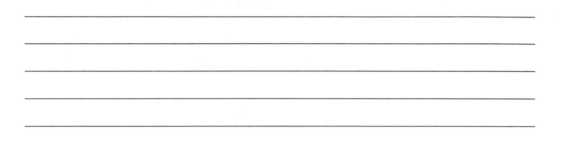

3. What is the appropriate role for students?

Perhaps an even more important issue to be considered here concerns one's personal view of who students are. It is widely assumed that educators all have a core value that speaks to the centrality of the needs of pupils as the driving force in schools. Although this may sound appealing and "right," is it truly your vision and value?

4. What is the appropriate role for teachers?

Again, the question might revolve around your personal definition of who teachers are in the first place. Some people view teachers as true professionals who have the best interests of their students in mind as they proceed with their duties. Others view teachers as district employees who can be replaced easily with others who have the same certification and academic degrees. Are these views consistent with your perspective, or do you have other notions of who teachers are and what they should be doing in schools?

_____

_____

_____

5. What is the appropriate role for parents and other community members?

Most schools greet visitors with a sign or decal on the front door with a statement such as, "This is your school—and welcome to it." But do you mean that? Are parents truly partners in the educational program, or are they intruders? What about the great majority of community members out there who pay taxes but who do not have children enrolled in your [or any other] school? What about your views on private businesses in your community?

6. What is my personal definition of "curriculum"?

Modern definitions of effective principals note that they are instructional, or curricular, leaders. What does this mean in practice? Part of it must be based on one's ability to have a clear personal understanding of what the curriculum is and what it should be in a particular school setting. For example, how inclusive should a school's curriculum be?

_____

_____

_____

_____

_____

7. What do I want this school to become?

What is your personal vision for the school? What kind of hopes and dreams for a more effective school drive your work? What are your ideals?

_____

_____

_____

_____

_____

_____

8. How will I know if students learned?

The ultimate goal of any school must be to ensure that learning has taken place among the students. But what are the indicators, at least in your mind, of whether or not this has really taken place? Some say that students' scores on stand-ardized achievement tests are valid indicators, whereas some say that learning really occurs only when established outcomes or performance indicators are reached. What is your answer?

_____

_____

_____

_____

_____

_____

9. How do I want others to see me?

It is important for a leader to reflect on the kinds of images that he or she projects to followers. How do you hope that you will be viewed by your teachers, staff, students, and community members? Think about this issue in two ways: as a principal, and also as a person.

_____

_____

_____

_____

_____

_____

10. What are my nonnegotiable values?

This last question might be the single most important issue to be addressed in your platform. Ultimately, this question asks you to consider the kinds of things that, if violated by the system or by other people with whom you must work, would cause you to "throw your keys on the table" and seek employment elsewhere.

What Do You Do With the Platform?

The value in an educational platform is not found by simply writing it out one time, putting it in a file cabinet, and then letting it sit for the rest of your professional life. Rather, it should be seen as a living document or statement regarding the parameters that you will put around different decisions made in your career. Platforms will change as you move through your professional life. For example, your thinking about the desirability of standardized testing as a way to measure student growth and progress may change drastically from today until some point in your future. The vision of "perfect" teachers may be modified greatly as you move farther away from your days in that same role.

We believe that the development of a formal statement of values through the educational platform has many important applications that can be of great assistance to you as you travel through your career as an educational leader. For one thing, developing clarity regarding your nonnegotiable values—even though these might change in the future—can be a genuine help to you as you think about making changes in jobs, moving to other districts, accepting transfers within the school system, and so forth. For example, we know many colleagues who have turned their backs on higher salaries and more prestigious jobs because taking those positions would cause them to compromise more important or professional values, such as being able to stay home with family more, or continuing to work with students from populations needing attention.

Second, the articulation of a clear statement of an educational platform is a value to those with whom you are to work, both at your individual school site and also coworkers across your district. We do not advocate printing multiple copies of your platform and then sending them around to everyone you might meet (or nailing it to the cathedral door!). However, we have found that people who have taken the time to write their platforms from time to time inevitably have a stronger grasp of their own values, so that those around them are also able to see what "makes them tick." This not only has the benefit of enabling principals to be open to their staffs, but it is also a powerful way to model communication skills that lead to a more effective school in general. In the long run, too, becoming more clear about your personal educational values will assist you in those cases where you may seek other professional positions. For example, an opening for a principalship in another school district that seems more prestigious or offers more in terms of salary might not be nearly as desirable once you consider the possible compromises that may be needed with regard to your personal values.

Finally, the ultimate value of developing a clear statement of an educational platform may be that it can serve as the foundation for long-term professional development. Too often, we have seen educators simply drift through their careers and engage in sporadic and periodic programs of professional growth and development based largely on learning more about one "hot topic" or another, or because the central office has made it clear that "all principals ought to jump on this or that bandwagon." In many cases, principals simply respond to the visions or platforms of others. We believe that it would be far more desirable for principals to engage in systematic career planning that is rooted in their own values and sense of where they are going or what is important to them. It is for this reason that we often suggest that people begin their professional development portfolios with a clear statement of their platforms. In that way, other elements of the portfolio are able to flow in a logical sequence from a strong foundation.

Your Personal Plan

In the next few pages, we suggest that you begin to sketch out some of the more critical elements of your own educational platform as a way to lead remaining elements of your personal portfolio and growth plan. You may wish to consult and respond to the questions posed earlier, or you may respond to other critical issues that will provide a greater sense of who you are as a professional educator.

_____

_____

_____

_____

_____

_____

_____

_____

_____

_____

_____

_____

Now that you have written the "planks" of your platform, the last step in this self-improvement process involves a clear statement of what you plan to do to implement your personal vision of effective practice. Once you have completed this last step, we suggest that a final valuable activity involves sharing your statements with one or two close friends, family members, or colleagues with a simple request to indicate whether or not they recognize you through the words that are on paper. If not, you may wish to reconsider some of what you have written to decide whether or not you have written a "real" or "ideal" description.

4

Being a "Boss"

SHARON MITCHELL was really excited last summer when she got the word that she had been selected as the new principal of O'Hare Elementary School, a small building with a great reputation for extremely effective teachers and very supportive parents. As a teacher at the Midway School located only a few blocks from O'Hare, Sharon was able to see what was going on in her new school. She was always impressed with the place, and now she felt she had "died and gone to heaven" when she learned that her first administrative job would be at O'Hare.

Soon after she moved into her new office in early July, Sharon began to realize that being a principal carried a lot of responsibilities not generally covered in the official school district policy manual or established job description. Further, she saw quickly that the courses she had completed for state principal certification at Meiggs University had not really provided her with a complete picture of her new school or her job as a principal.

For example, she quickly understood that now that she was the principal, people reacted to her quite differently. She had known most of the teachers at O'Hare for many years. But now, as they began to come back to get their classrooms ready for the start of the next school year, she could feel a distinct chill in the air. She was now "Mrs. Mitchell" to many who had referred to her simply as "Sharon" in the past. It now seemed like a major production just to get out of her building at the same time each day so that she could get home to prepare dinner for her family, a task she now looked forward to because it reminded her of a time last year when she could really get something accomplished in a predictable way. And the smiling folks at the central office who said so many supportive things during the job interview process were beginning to make it increasingly clear that she would be treated like all the other principals in the district, even though most other administrators had at least 6 years of experience in their roles. Finally, Sharon was becoming weary of the seemingly endless parade of parents and other community members who came to her door on a daily basis with "just one more simple little question" or request, often issues and requests that had been denied by the former principal. But Sharon was new on the scene, and many people wanted to test her resolve about a variety of issues.

The school year had just begun, and Sharon was not completely certain that she would be able to make it to Halloween!

* * *

When people take their first principalships, the reaction and situation are often not very different from the scenario described above. Being named as a school principal may be the fulfillment of a long-standing ambition. All the conditions associated with a particular position might be quite favorable in terms of the location of a school, an individual's feeling of comfort with the school, the reputation of the teachers, and so forth. Even with all these factors going the right way, however, it is impossible to ignore that when you become a principal for the first time, you will face certain issues. One of these is that people will look at you differently, expect different things from you, and hold you accountable in ways that will be markedly different from what they did in the past. Simply stated, you are now "the boss," and this designation carries certain challenges and demands. Once again, this fact reinforces the theme that we described in the previous chapter, namely that a critical skill for beginners must be a recognition of how the job of being a principal is related to your own sense of self.

No matter how well prepared you may feel as you move into a formal leadership role for the first time, we believe that it is impossible to escape the fact that being the boss brings with it certain pressures and demands. This chapter will identify some of the kinds of things that are likely to face any newcomer during the first part of the transition into the principal's office. If you have already served in the capacity of an assistant principal, you have no doubt had some insights into these issues, although there is still no substitute for serving as the top administrator in a school. When the weight of full responsibility for an organization falls on your shoulders, it is very different from serving as an assistant.

The chapter also includes some practical hints for helping you increase your self-awareness and feelings of identity so that you can meet the pressures of leadership with greater confidence.

Others' Perceptions

As Sharon Mitchell discovered very quickly in our opening scenario, one of the things that changes almost immediately when you become a principal is the way in which other people see you. Of course, you don't feel a lot different from the way you were just a few weeks ago. Admittedly, you may now be considerably more tired and you may often feel that there are not enough hours in a day to provide you with the time needed to carry out your new job. But down deep, you know that you are still the same person you have been for your whole life. It's just that people around you—teachers, office and custodial staff, parents, and students—perceive you differently and interact differently with you. Although we are not suggesting that you should deliberately try to change, you need to recognize that the perceptions of others can be powerful forces that will affect you directly, or will affect the ways in which *other* people will see you. And in the long run, these are the kinds of things that will enable you to be more effective as a school principal.

Before we list some of the ways in which we believe beginning principals are perceived differently by people who work with them, if you are currently in your first year as a principal (or if you talk with people who are now beginning principals), list some of the ways in which you have noticed people treating "the rookie principal" differently from the way they did in the past. (For example, do people appear to be less inclined to talk openly with you about some of their professional concerns now?)

_____

_____

_____

_____

_____

_____

Researchers have noted that beginning principals receive signals from teachers, colleague administrators, parents (and other community members), students, and immediate family members that suggest that they are somehow different now that they are the boss.

Teachers, even in these days of increased empowerment and efforts to promote opportunities for involvement in decision making, still tend to look toward someone being "in charge." As a result, we believe that the role of the formal school leader may change somewhat in tone (perhaps from "director" to "facilitator"). But we also believe that when you are the principal of a school, people will continue to look at you as a person who will make critical decisions in times of need. You are an authority figure who has the right to make critical decisions, and people know that. What is often difficult to remember, however, is that each teacher has a very strong sense of when the "time of need" is to arise. Some staff members will rarely come directly to you as the principal to make decisions for them. On the other hand, every school will have a teacher or two (or more) who will rely on you as the boss to tell them what should be done about even seemingly insignificant issues ("Would it be all right for me to open a few windows in my classroom, even though it's raining?").

A second aspect of becoming the boss relates to the idea implied by the often-cited sign on President Truman's desk: "The buck stops here." When you are in charge of something, whether it is a small elementary school, a large high school, or a huge school district, you are the person who is ultimately responsible for the effective operation of that organization. You cannot make a mistake and then blame it on someone else. Having made that last statement, however, we are aware that there are principals who tend to attribute any unpopular decision to the fact that "the central office made me do it," or "we have to because the state requires it." We note here that such principals are typically not respected by their administrative peers, and they are typically not very effective leaders.

Another price that novice principals often report is that they suddenly feel very alone in their school systems. It is ironic that in many cases, individuals move into administrative positions within their school systems largely because they are recognized as people with great interpersonal and social skills; their peers like and admire them. Often, they are at the center of professional and social gatherings, leading many to assume that they will carry these skills into the principal's office. Many newcomers are then amazed to find out that, as one new principal once told us, they have "crossed the line" separating themselves from their teacher friends when they became a principal. We are often reminded of a quote from another new principal several years ago who observed, "Last year, when I was still a teacher and I walked into the teachers' lounge, I was the center of attention and had a chance to talk with everyone. This year, as the principal, I walk into that same lounge and there's dead silence. Same school, same teachers, same me. But people used to talk with me; now, I know that they talk about me."

So What Do You Do?

We have pointed out that people will start to look at you very differently when you take on the role of principal. People react to this fact in a number of ways, some of which may be quite unproductive. For example, we often see new principals discovering that their teachers are not engaging them in the ways that they did in the past. Their reaction might be to decide to put the teachers out of their lives in many ways. They begin to build walls and isolate themselves. Soon, principals who adopt this stance begin to spend most of their time in their offices or out of their buildings. A common symptom of this situation beginning to develop involves the principal beginning to view things in terms of "us" (or "me") versus "them," with "them" being all teachers.

Another behavioral pattern often adopted by principals who sense separation from their teaching staffs is the tendency to begin to internalize everything and make it their sole responsibility. They stop delegating even small tasks. The result can be very unfortunate, as principals begin to feel increasing stress that they do not have the time to do everything, they have no friends, they cannot rely on anyone, they have no one to help them do their jobs, and so forth.

A third approach seen in some beginning principals faced with the sense that they are no longer accepted by their teaching colleagues is to take on a deliberate stance of being officious. They hide behind rules, regulations, policies, procedures, and anything else that might serve to depersonalize their jobs. In this way, they can develop the sense that they are not involved with people who are rejecting them. Their stance is one of coming to work, following rules, avoiding contact whenever possible, and then going home from work without worrying about the people with whom they work. They tend not to be very happy people on the job, to say the least.

Finally, some new principals deal with their sense of separation from teachers in a very different way. In many cases, they begin to reject their roles as administrators and strive to appear as if they are still part of the teaching team. Although this may not at first sound like a problem—*after all, isn't it good to still be a teacher?*—there are some major difficulties that will inevitably arise when beginning principals avoid becoming a "boss." It is important to remember, for example, that a major responsibility of a principal is the evaluation of staff, often with the result being an unhappy decision related to a person's career. Although we do not wish to suggest that principals avoid contact with their teachers only because they may have to evaluate them negatively some day, we also wish to note that some distance between teachers and administrators may not be totally undesirable.

The fact is, regardless of how you may wish to deal with it, the step you have taken from your former life as a teacher into administration means that certain relationships will change and that new expectations and demands will naturally follow you into your new role. But that sort of transition does not have to be traumatic or cause the kinds of negative behaviors we have noted above. As one principal told us, "When you become a principal, you have to remember that you are still part of the family that you were a member of before. But now, you are the head of that family. Your job now becomes one of doing all that you can to promote the well-being of everyone. You can't be a 'buddy,' but you have to be a friend in the truest sense." Differences do not necessarily mean that you care less for everyone in the family. The trick of administration often is to demonstrate your caring about others through the establishment of trust. When you achieve that level of interaction, differences between you—*the boss*—and the teachers—*the employees*—will begin to disappear. In short, if you want separation, you can find it. On the other hand, if you want effective teamwork, you have to work on that, too, but it can be achieved.

We do not deny that being in charge of any organization can be stressful and can serve to make a person feel alone and even rejected by others from time to time. This is particularly true in those cases where people are promoted from within; one day they work with a group of people, but the next day they are "making those same people work for them." Nevertheless, we believe that there are things that can be done to reduce the sense of separation one feels and that the ways that we noted earlier are not good choices. Your job is not to agonize over the sense of separation, but to promote a sense of unity in your school.

What are some of the ways in which you have addressed the issue of feeling apart from your teachers, now that you've "crossed the line" and become "the boss"? (For example, some principals promote monthly "sharing sessions" where they invite their teachers to spend half an hour or so talking about professional concerns that they are facing.)

Strategies to Reduce Isolation

We suggest that the best way to help you in reducing your sense of becoming isolated as the boss involves making links with key people in and outside of your building.

Inside your building, it is critical that you build bridges with a few key individuals who can serve as sounding boards for you throughout the school year. This is not always an easy task. It is nearly impossible to tell who can be trusted as a confidant when you first walk into a new school. This is particularly true if you are new to the school district, and you have no clear idea of who the players are going to be. Nevertheless, it is essential to find allies in your immediate environment. If you are in an elementary school or a fairly small secondary school, it is likely that the first person who will come to your mind as a person to be trusted is the secretary for the school. She or he will likely know more about the "real issues" that face your school than just about anyone else that you will first encounter.

The only thing that needs to be safeguarded in such situations, of course, is the possibility that "insights" into what and who are important in your new school might be clouded by only one person's perceptions. Also, there is a possibility that well-intentioned conversations about key people in your school might become opportunities for gossip and hearsay. Secretaries have great insights into what is going on in schools. On the other hand, they often do not know all the reasons why people behave in the ways that they do at times.

If you happen to work in a school where there are assistant principals, these individuals might also serve as natural members of your "inner circle" of confidants. There are, of course, some restrictions to this suggestion. For example, finding out that one or more of your assistants was an unsuccessful applicant for your job might make that person questionable as an ongoing supporter. Also, you may quickly determine that one of the things that you must do in your principalship is to encourage your assistant principal to seek other opportunities for professional advancement. In other words, one of the things that you may need to do is to find a new assistant principal. Despite these reservations, however, reliance on assistant principals as sources of important information regarding your new school can be an effective way to reduce your sense of isolation from "what is really going on."

A third potential source of support internal to your school will be a few teachers with whom you can feel comfortable in opening up and sharing some personal concerns. Again, these people will not be visible at first as you move into a school. In the long run, however, it is important that you spend the time and effort needed to find teachers who can be trusted on a continuing basis. Remember, too, that those who come forward in the first few days of your new administrative role are often the last persons who will become enduring supporters. In this regard, we simply suggest that you rely on experiences that you had as a classroom teacher. Eventually, each class has a few students who become close allies of the teacher. The same can be said of the dynamics in any teaching staff that you join. Incidentally, this is one of those places where a firm appreciation and understanding of your educational platform will be a critical part of your success. How do you look at teachers, for example? As you think through your responses to this issue, your relationships with a few valued colleagues will emerge.

Finally, as you try to assess key issues and other aspects of the internal realities of your school, do not forget that in many cases, you will have inherited a structure for operating your school that may be quite helpful. It is likely that there are already in place committees and task forces that were formed prior to your arrival. Spending some time with members of these groups can be an important tool for you as you try to develop a comprehensive and positive picture of what's going on.

If these types of work groups don't already exist, you may think about announcing that you want nominations of staff to serve on a building "Steering Committee" or "Instructional Improvement Committee." As people are identified by others as possible candidates for this work, you will develop not only a strong core of people with whom you may be able to work on a variety of projects, but you will also gain insights into which people in your school are perceived by their peers as leaders.

As you think about your present school, who might be included as members of your inner circle of confidants? (Will you include your secretary? Assistant principal? Team leaders? A teacher or two with whom you used to work when you were in the classroom?)

Your Personal Plan

Again, the issues we have reviewed in this chapter deal with the area of self-awareness or role awareness skills as one of the concerns of beginning administrators. In this section, we suggest that you write down some of your thoughts related to frustrations that you are now experiencing because you are the boss in your school. These frustrations might be linked to the items we have identified earlier, or they might be unique concerns that you have found related to your first job as a school principal. In either case, we encourage you to include these issues as part of the process of building your own personal portfolio and growth plan. It is our assumption that unless you identify some of these issues, you will never be able to deal effectively with them. For each item listed as a frustration, we also suggest that you indicate some of the ways in which you have been able to cope with it and proceed with your work as an educational leader.

5

A Personal Leadership Checkup

TOM CASEY was enjoying his first year as the principal of Avon Hills High School. For the past 3 years, he was one of the assistant principals in the school, and he had the opportunity to learn about the teachers, students, parents, and other members of the community. It was not a surprise when Tom was named the principal; he knew the school and the school community knew him.

As Tom moved through his first year, he remained quite comfortable with his assignment, for the most part. It was a continuation of what he did in the past, and things seemed to be running smoothly. On the other hand, Tom often went home at the end of the day feeling as if there was something missing from this year's experience. He wasn't completely confident about how he was doing as a leader. He was sure that others watching his performance would say that he was a good principal. Avon Hills was "working" pretty well, but the principal wished that he could start to get some sense of how well he was really doing as a leader.

*   *   *

Tom Casey is not unusual. Too often, beginning principals invest so much time in finding their first job, getting the school year started, and keeping their buildings open and well-maintained that they have little or no opportunity to check out the effectiveness of their work. Are they doing a good job? Or are they simply staying one step ahead of the next crisis that will land on their desks? School districts, of course, have timelines and procedures to be followed in the evaluation of their administrative personnel. However, these evaluative procedures are often cast in a way that is tied to either merit pay decisions or determining contract extensions. Typical evaluation practices for school administrators are designed to assess whether or not people are doing their jobs, not whether or not they are growing professionally and becoming more effective leaders. The result is that principals, whether at the beginning of their careers or with much experience, rarely get any insights into the effectiveness of their work during the school year. We believe that this is unfortunate because it promotes the notion that principals, particularly those new to the job, are meant to direct their efforts toward survivorship, not leadership.

In this chapter, we provide you with an opportunity to reflect on your own leadership style and skills, as compared with the nature of effective educational leadership that is widely represented in the current research literature. The most important part of this process involves the expectation that you will conclude your review of the material presented in this chapter by identifying some of your particular strengths and weaknesses. In turn, these may serve as yet another part of your personal professional development portfolio. Our goal here is not to indicate those areas where you have problems. Rather, we want you to be clear about the ways in which you can enhance your role as an educational leader.

Critical Leadership Skills

The number of lists that exist and contain statements of specific skills reported to be needed by effective leaders is probably almost as long as the number of people who have been appointed as leaders over the years. Some of the existing lists we include that might be of relevance to our discussion are those prepared by the Association for Supervision and Curriculum Development (ASCD; 1989), Stephen Covey (1991), Warren Bennis (Bennis & Nanus, 1985), the National Association of Elementary School Principals (NAESP; 1991), and the National Association of Secondary School Principals (NASSP; Schmitt, Noe, Meritt, Fitzgerald, & Jorgensen, 1982).

The ASCD list notes that effective educational leaders

1. *Provide a sense of vision to their schools.* They demonstrate the ability to articulate what a school is supposed to do, particularly in terms of what it should do to benefit children.

2. *Engage in participative management.* They encourage a better organizational climate in the school by allowing teachers and staff to participate meaningfully in real decision making, and not merely in an effort to "play at" getting people to be involved when decisions are already made.

3. *Provide support for instruction.* Instructional leaders are so committed to maintaining quality instruction as their primary organizational focus that when decisions must be made concerning priorities, instruction always comes first.

4. *Monitor instruction.* They know what is going on in the classrooms of their schools.

5. *Are resourceful.* Instructional leaders rarely allow circumstances in their organizations to get in the way of their vision for quality educational programs.

Stephen Covey, a professor at Brigham Young University, has noted the following characteristics of what he refers to as "Principle-Centered Leaders."

1. *They are continually learning.* Principle-centered people are constantly educated by their experiences.

2. *They are service oriented.* Those striving to be principle-centered see life as a mission.

3. *They radiate positive energy.* Principle-centered people are cheerful, pleasant, and happy.

4. *They believe in other people.* Principle-centered people don't overreact to negative behaviors, criticism, or human weaknesses.

5. *They lead balanced lives.* They read the best literature and magazines and keep up with current affairs and events.

6. *They see life as an adventure.* Principle-centered people savor life; they have no need to categorize or stereotype people and events.

7. *They are synergistic.* Principle-centered people serve as change catalysts in organizations, and they improve most situations in which they become involved.

8. *They exercise for self-renewal.* They regularly exercise the four dimensions of the human personality: physical, mental, emotional, and spiritual.

Warren Bennis has noted that successful leaders engage in the following five strategies.

1. *Strategy I: Attention Through Vision.* Leaders develop a focus in an organization, or an agenda, that demonstrates an unparalleled concern for outcomes, products, and results.

2. *Strategy II: Meaning Through Communication.* Effective communication is inseparable from effective leadership.

3. *Strategy III: Trust Through Positioning.* Leaders must be trusted in order to be effective; we trust people who are predictable, and whose positions are known. Leaders who are trusted make themselves known and make their positions clear.

4. *Strategy IV: The Deployment of Self Through Positive Self-Regard.* Leaders have positive self-images, self-regard that is not self-centered, and they know their worth. In general, they are confident without being cocky.

5. *Strategy V: The Deployment of Self Through the "Wallenda Factor."* Before his death, the famous aerialist Karl Wallenda was said to have become more preoccupied with not falling than with succeeding. Leaders are able consistently to focus their energies on success.

After reading these lists of critical skills for leaders identified by ASCD, Stephen Covey, and Warren Bennis, select two or three skills that you believe are things others would identify in your style of work as a school principal:

_____

_____

_____

_____

_____

_____

Now, review the three lists again and select two or three skills that you believe might be identified as shortcomings in your style:

_____

_____

_____

_____

_____

_____

Another listing of critical leadership skills has been developed by the National Association of Elementary School Principals (NAESP). This group of skills is somewhat different from the others we have reviewed because it has been designed in a way that may enable an individual school principal to review what he or she might believe to be skills in need of further refinement and improvement. As you consider each leadership area, take time to assess your own performance in this area as a critical component of your work:

Area 1: Leadership Behavior

The principal must:

1. Exercise vision and provide leadership that appropriately involves staff, students, and the community in the identification and accomplishment of the school's mission.

   Your level of personal proficiency in this skill:

   _____

   _____

2. Recognize the individual needs of all staff and students, including those who are at risk because of diverse cultures, backgrounds, and abilities.

   Your personal level of proficiency in this skill:

   _____

   _____

3. Apply effective human relations skills.

   Your personal level of proficiency in this skill:

   _____

   _____

4. Encourage and develop the leadership of others.

   Your personal level of proficiency in this skill:

   _____

   _____

5. Analyze relevant information, make decisions, delegate responsibility, and provide appropriate support and follow-up.

   Your level of personal proficiency in this skill:

   _____

   _____

6. Identify and creatively coordinate the use of available human, material, and financial resources to achieve the school's mission and goals.

Your level of personal proficiency in this skill:

_____

_____

7. Explore, assess, develop, and implement educational concepts that enhance teaching and learning.

   Your level of personal proficiency in this skill:

_____

_____

8. Bond the school community through shared values and beliefs.

   Your level of personal proficiency in this skill:

_____

_____

9. Initiate and manage constructive change.

   Your level of personal proficiency in this skill:

_____

_____

10. Participate actively as a member of local, state, and national professional groups.

    Your level of personal proficiency in this skill:

_____

_____

Area 2: Communication Skills

The principal must:

1. Articulate beliefs persuasively, effectively defend decisions, explain innovations, and behave in ways that are congruent with these beliefs and decisions.

   Your level of personal proficiency in this skill:

_____

_____

2. Write clearly and concisely so that the message is understood by the intended audience.

   Your level of personal proficiency in this skill:

   _____

   _____

3. Utilize basic facts and data and recognize values when communicating priorities.

   Your level of personal proficiency in this skill:

   _____

   _____

4. Demonstrate skills in nonverbal communication, including personal impact, to communicate a positive image of the school.

   Your level of personal proficiency in this skill:

   _____

   _____

5. Use current technologies to communicate the school's philosophy, mission, needs, and accomplishments.

   Your level of personal proficiency in this skill:

   _____

   _____

6. Make effective use of mass media.

   Your level of personal proficiency in this skill:

   _____

   _____

7. Use active listening skills.

   Your level of personal proficiency in this skill:

   _____

   _____

8. Express disagreement without being disagreeable.

   Your level of personal proficiency in this skill:

   _____

   _____

9. Promote student and staff use of higher-level thinking skills.

   Your level of personal proficiency in this skill:

   _____

   _____

10. Exemplify the behavior expected in others.

    Your level of personal proficiency in this skill:

    _____

    _____

11. Keep communication flowing to and from the school.

    Your level of personal proficiency in this skill:

    _____

    _____

12. Communicate effectively with the various constituencies within the school community.

    Your level of personal proficiency in this skill:

    _____

    _____

Area 3: Group Processes

The principal must:

1. Apply the principles of group dynamics and facilitation skills.

   Your level of personal proficiency in this skill:

   _____

   _____

2. Involve staff, parents, students, and the community in setting goals.

   Your level of personal proficiency in this skill:

   _____

   _____

3. Resolve difficult situations by use of conflict resolution skills.

   Your level of personal proficiency in this skill:

   _____

   _____

4. Match the appropriate decision-making techniques to the particular situation.

   Your level of personal proficiency in this skill:

   _____

   _____

5. Identify—in collaboration with staff, parents, and students—the decision-making procedures the school will follow.

   Your level of personal proficiency in this skill:

   _____

   _____

6. Apply the process of consensus building both as a leader and as a member of a group.

   Your level of personal proficiency in this skill:

   _____

   _____

7. Achieve intended outcomes through the use of principles of motivation.

   Your level of personal proficiency in this skill:

   _____

   _____

In addition to these proficiencies related to the leadership responsibilities of school principals, NAESP suggests that you may wish to review your performance in the following areas as well.

Supervisory Proficiencies

1. Curriculum
2. Instruction
3. Performance
4. Evaluation

Administrative and Management Competencies

1. Organizational management
2. Fiscal management
3. Political management

One additional framework that we present is derived from the Assessment Center skill areas identified by the National Association of Secondary School Principals (NASSP). We believe that a periodic review of the extent to which you are demonstrating these competencies may be an important and useful technique to guide your personal leadership checkup.

Administrative Skill Dimensions

1. *Problem analysis:* the ability to seek out relevant data and analyze complex information to determine the important elements of a problem situation, searching for information with a purpose
2. *Judgment:* the ability to reach logical conclusions and make high-quality decisions based on available information; skill in identifying educational needs and setting priorities; ability to critically evaluate communications
3. *Organizational ability:* the ability to plan, schedule, and control the work of others; skill in using resources in an optimal fashion; ability to deal with a volume of paperwork and heavy demands on one's time
4. *Leadership:* the ability to get others involved in solving problems; ability to recognize when a group requires direction; ability to interact effectively with a group to guide them to accomplish a task

5. *Sensitivity* (the ability to perceive the needs, concerns, and personal problems of others; tact in dealing with persons from different backgrounds; ability to deal effectively with people concerning emotional issues; knowing what information to communicate and to whom)

6. *Decisiveness* (the ability to recognize when a decision is required and to act quickly)

7. *Range of interests* (competence to discuss a variety of subjects—educational, political, current events, economic, etc.; active participation in events)

8. *Personal motivation* (the need to achieve in all activities; evidence that work is important to personal satisfaction; ability to be self-policing)

9. *Educational values* (possession of a well-reasoned education; philosophy; reactiveness to new ideas)

10. *Stress tolerance* (the ability to perform under pressure and during opposition; the ability to think on one's feet)

11. *Oral communication* (the ability to make clear oral presentations of facts or ideas)

12. *Written communication* (the ability to express ideas clearly in writing; to write appropriately for different audiences—students, parents, etc.)

13. *Conflict management* (the willingness to intervene in conflict situations and the ability to develop solutions that are agreeable to all persons involved)

14. *Political astuteness* (the ability to perceive critical features of the environment such as power structure, principal players, and special interest groups; the ability to formulate alternatives that reflect realistic expectations)

15. *Risk taking* (the extent to which calculated risks are taken based on sound judgments)

16. *Creativity* (the ability to generate ideas that provide new and different solutions to management problems or opportunities)

As you read through these 16 competence areas, in which areas do you believe you would like to focus some attention for personal improvement?

_____

_____

_____

_____

_____

_____

For each of those areas in which you would like to improve your performance, what are some specific strategies that you might follow as part of a plan for personal improvement? (For example, if one of the skill areas identified for improvement is written communication, you may wish to enroll in a writing course at a local college, or simply ask a friend to critique your written memos, letters, and so forth.)

_____

_____

_____

_____

_____

_____

Your Personal Plan

An assessment of your leadership skills can serve as an important foundation for a personal portfolio and growth plan. In the space below, identify some of your strengths and also some of your weaknesses with regard to the leadership skills identified throughout this chapter. For each item, identify a timeline that you intend to follow in either strengthening that skill or finding ways to increase your personal skills. Also, note some of the activities or strategies you believe may assist you in your improvement efforts. (For example, "I will increase the effectiveness of my public speaking or oral communication skills over the next school year by participating in the local Toastmaster's Club and also by volunteering often to make public addresses.")

_____

_____

_____

_____

_____

References

Association for Supervision and Curriculum Development. (1989). *Instructional leadership* [Videotape]. Alexandria, VA: Author.

Bennis, W. & Nanus, B. (1985). *Leaders: The strategies for taking charge.* New York: Harper & Row.

Covey, S. R. (1991). *Principle-centered leadership.* New York: Simon & Schuster.

National Association of Elementary School Principals. (1991). *Proficiencies for principals* (Rev. ed.). Alexandria, VA: Author.

Schmitt, N., Joe, R., Meritt, R., Fitzgerald, M., & Jorgensen, C. (1982). *Criterion-related and content validity of the NASSP Assessment Center.* Reston, VA: Author.

6

Expectations for Technical and Managerial Skills

NATE SPENCER stood at the front door of Martin Avenue Elementary School with a key to the building in his right hand, suddenly realizing that, at least for the next year of his life, he would be the principal of this school. This was a job that he had looked forward to obtaining for quite a while. Last spring, Nate applied for principalships that were advertised as open in five different school districts close to where he had been a teacher for the past 11 years. In total, Nate went through 12 interviews with different groups of parents, teachers, central office administrators, community group representatives, students, and, in a few cases, school board members. In some cases, he had done well, and in a few situations, he had really "bombed out." In any case, when he finally got a phone call to take over at Martin Avenue, he leaped at the chance to prove that he could do a great job as a principal.

Today, however, he started to get some feelings of apprehension as he walked through the front door of his new school. He had learned a lot from his administrative internship last year, a requirement for administrative certification through Wheatland University. He had a particularly good role model in a principal who worked with him during that period. Nate also felt as if he had learned some very practical information while he was taking graduate courses at Wheatland. Now, however, he realized that he was in charge and that he was responsible for "making things happen" at his school. As he settled in at his new desk, he started to sift through the enormous pile of papers that were laid neatly in his in-basket by Maria Delvechio, his secretary. She now stood before him, notebook in hand, waiting for directions concerning what might be the next order of business to be followed during the next few weeks as the school year was about to start. Maria suggested that one of the first things she had always done with the previous principals was to set up a tentative schedule or calendar to be followed during the school year.

That way, both she and Nate could develop a "tickler file" that they could consult each day to remind them of big events that needed to be addressed as the year progressed.

Nate thought that Maria had a great idea, but the newness of the job, the thought of being "the boss," and all the assorted things that had to be done to learn about a new school, a new school system, and a new job made Nate realize that he had not given any thought in the past to what had to be done in terms of technical skills and practices needed to make this a successful first year on the job.

* * *

Nate's situation is not unique. Often, people spend so much time thinking about how to do individual tasks associated with the principalship (e.g., how to manage a building budget, or how to observe and evaluate teachers, or how to pay attention to legal mandates) that they never think in terms of the "big picture" of leading a school for an entire year. They also frequently find themselves in situations much like Nate's: They spend a lot of time worrying about and working toward getting their first job and often walk into the position without really considering a lot of the details of what they are supposed to do. These are both realistic situations beginners often face, and they are concerns not remembered by experienced colleagues who often do things based on their experience.

Some Apparent Contradictions

Throughout this book, we have emphasized that the most critical skills that must be addressed by anyone in the beginning phases of a career as a principal are associated with developing an appreciation of personal values and beliefs, and also the ability to "fit" into a new social setting. Although we will not back away from that view, this chapter might seem contradictory because it looks at the important areas of technical and managerial skills needed for principals to succeed in their jobs. Often, people speak of administrative technical skills in a negative way; they talk about the "Three B's of School Administration: Beans, Buses, and Budgets." The implication is that being an effective school leader is something well beyond mere management. Again, we agree with that view, but we also know that a person can never serve as a true leader if he or she does not also survive as a manager. The job has to be done.

In this chapter, we look at the technical and managerial side of the principal's job. Our goal here is to present an overview of the many tasks that need to be done each year by school principals by working with you to set up a kind of schedule for carrying out these various tasks. Some of the items might be classified as formal or mandated activities that are required by state law, collective bargaining agreements, or local school board policy. Exact dates will vary in different school districts or states. There are also other important technical duties that need to be done by effective principals, even if they are not officially required.

Formal Requirements

There are a number of things that you must do each year because they are formal requirements of the job. If you miss deadlines associated with carrying out these types of tasks, you may be in violation of contracts, local policies, or even state and local laws. As a result, these items cannot be allowed to simply slip once in a while. You could lose your job or be held personally and legally liable if you do not meet these kinds of deadlines and due dates.

We certainly do not wish to minimize the importance of these formally defined deadlines and activities. However, in most cases, you will not have a hard time learning these dates each year. They are listed in formal memos, the district's weekly calendar of events, job descriptions, board policies, and a wide array of other places that will make them relatively hard to ignore. Few principals are wholly unprepared for the fact that, for example, they must complete the evaluations of nontenured teachers in their buildings by a certain date. This is an important technical and managerial task that you must address, but it is not a subtle issue that is easy to forget most of the time.

Informal Tasks

These are the things that you will not necessarily find listed in the local school district's board policy manual, or in the school code for your state, or even in the terms of the negotiated contract for your local teachers' association. However, failing to do some of these things might make a difference in how you are able to carry out your job as a principal. They are the kinds of things that—as experienced principals have discovered over the years—make the school year run a bit more smoothly and reduce tension and frustrations not only for you but also in your staff, students, and the community with whom you will work.

In the next few pages, we will list some of the important things—both formal and informal—that need to be done throughout the school year. Our lists indicate activities that should be performed before the year begins, during the year, and toward the end of the school year to ensure that next year will be easier than this one was. Some of our suggestions fit nicely and cleanly into one of these three periods; others do not because they must be addressed throughout the year.

Before the Year Begins

Most people get their first administrative assignments during the summer, before the new school year begins. In an ideal world, you might be selected as a principal in May or June, with an understanding that your contract officially begins on July 1 and that teachers will be back by mid-August, 2 or 3 weeks before students arrive for the beginning of the first year in which you are a principal. In that ideal world, then, you might have a few months to plan for the next year; check over your new school; learn about the students, teachers, staff, and school district; and so forth. In the real world, however, many receive their first principalships only a few weeks (or days) before the next school year begins.

Regardless of the situation in which you find yourself, there are a number of things that can be done in the months, weeks, or even days before the teachers and students walk into your school. We classify these activities in several different areas: building preparation; materials and supplies; communications with staff, parents, community, and students; curriculum; and finally, perhaps most critically, personal preparation.

Building Preparation Activities

Some of the following activities may help you to prepare for your first year in the principalship:

- Walk around your school with your chief custodian and check out overall cleanliness and state of repair; notify custodial staff of areas needing attention.

- Examine lighting throughout the building.

- Look over such often-forgotten but important areas as ventilation, signs of water damage, plumbing problems, electrical problems, and so forth.

- Learn about your building fire alarm system and security systems (if any), and how to operate, override, and disconnect them if necessary.

- Verify that things ordered by the previous principal were actually done in your building for this year (e.g., were structural changes, repairs, etc. actually carried out by the custodial staff or contractors?).

- Check over the external conditions of your building during the summer months—and remember that the outside of your building, including the grounds around it, are what the public sees every day. (It never hurts to mow the lawn and make certain that weeds are pulled!)

- Update teacher and staff mail locations to reflect new staff members. (Remember that you're probably not going to be the only "new kid" in school next year. Making certain that little things like mailbox arrangements are taken care of is one way to avoid annoying teachers who are familiar with the way things are "supposed to be.")

- Learn your building's idiosyncrasies, hidden rooms, and so forth. (This is particularly an adventure in older buildings, or ones where several wings have been added over the years. Often, little closets are found in gyms, auditoriums, and other similar areas of schools.)

- Form a relationship with your district custodian supervisor or administrator. (This person can get you through some tough confrontations with reluctant custodians or repair people.)

- Do what you and your staff can to make the building as neat, clean, and attractive as possible for the first day that your teachers return. (This little step will have a big effect on morale!)

- Arrange your office so that it reflects you and your personal style: Move the desk, put up photos and plants, and so forth. (This strategy really tells new people a lot about you very quickly.)

Materials and Supplies

- Learn the location of supply closets, storage rooms, and so forth.

- Check to see if materials that were ordered last spring have been delivered this summer; if not, contact vendors to find out why not.

- Review purchasing procedures and forms required by the central office; meet with appropriate central office staff if necessary to learn more about local practices.

- Review supplies and materials inventory procedures.

- Make certain you have an ample supply of forms (e.g., budgeting forms, leave request forms, insurance forms, discipline referral forms, etc.) on hand to start the year so that you will not have to "bug" the central office for this material after the year starts.

- Make certain that such things as student and staff handbooks are ready to be distributed as soon as the new year begins.

Communications With Staff, Parents, Community, and Students

- Send out letters of introduction to parents and staff; invite people to stop by at the office to meet you during the summer. (This is particularly important for teachers who might not know much about you, where you came from, or a lot of other information that was not generally known by all teachers during the hiring process.)

- Take your building staff (secretaries, custodians) out to lunch, or at least make certain to spend a significant amount of one-on-one time with each of these very important people before the school year begins.

- Listen and learn as much as possible about the local culture of your school, your neighborhood, and the school district. Even if you came to this school from another building in the same district, this is an important tip.

- Meet with PTA/PTO officers, booster club officers, or any other organized parents' groups that will be a part of your school community.

- Work with experienced personnel to identify important local community groups, individuals, or organizations. (Do not offend important locals.)

- Identify important contact people in community social service agencies, the police department, and so forth. Find time to make personal visits to the people you may need to call on in emergencies after the year starts. (People will remember and always respond more quickly to requests from people they know.)

- Form business partnerships, if possible.

- Prepare a "Welcome Back" letter to parents and students and send it so that it will arrive a week or so before the school year officially begins. (And remember to proof this letter so that it contains no errors in spelling, punctuation, or grammar; you are "on stage" every time you send something out into the community!)

- Prepare a "Welcome Back" letter (and address it personally) to each teacher and staff member. (Talk about what you want to do in school, but *please*, avoid "educationese"!)

- Do not pass up invitations to important local and traditional events (the superintendent's cook-out, the teachers' family picnic, etc.) or seemingly unimportant community events (the annual pumpkin festival, etc.). Every one of these events is an opportunity to learn about the culture and show your sincere interest in the people who will be central to your success.

- Prepare the daily announcements and newsletters for the first week of the school year well in advance of the "big day." Also, prepare the agenda for your first staff meeting of the new year.

- Read local newspapers; subscribe to one if you live in another community.

Curriculum

- Learn the "teaching culture" of the school. Are teams used? Are there teachers who have always excelled as "loners"? Who works well with whom?

- Familiarize yourself with last year's test scores on any standardized measures; learn the schedule for administration for this next year.

- Review the district curriculum and graded course of study (if one exists); make certain that teachers have copies of, or at least access to, curriculum guides (as mandated by local or state policy).

- Learn about special education or inclusion programs that are followed in the district, and consider implications for your building.

- Meet with the district director of curriculum to learn additional specific characteristics of curriculum planning and development in your system.

Personal Preparation

- Read those journals that you previously put aside to learn about some major trends in education that you might be facing as a principal. (Many things seemed irrelevant to you as you reviewed them as a teacher; now, they may have major consequences for your leadership role.)

- Talk to people to learn about special school traditions, events, and customs.

- Set up a tentative monthly plan of events for next year. Set up a "tickler file" to remind you of significant deadlines or timelines that will need to be met or followed.

- Set up your personal phone filing system on your desk; set "speed dials" for frequent numbers.

- Visit with a few experienced local principals to set the stage for future collegial relations.

After the Year Starts

The temptation that you will face as the year begins is to settle in as the new principal and wait for issues to come to you. That will certainly happen. However, you must persist with making a plan that will enable you to anticipate some major events and crises that will happen to you as a new principal. Some of these things will take place at the beginning of the year, and some will come later. But be prepared.

Again, we list some of the common issues that you are likely to face throughout the year in a number of different areas.

Building and Physical Plant Activities

- Keep an eye out for any unusual signs of wear and tear on areas in the building, particularly as these might be related to the health and safety of students and staff.

- Carry out fire drills, tornado drills, and other forms of disaster drills, as required by local law and district policy.

- Make certain that custodial staff follow through on all assignments.

- Keep an eye on graffiti and vandalism around the school and make certain that, where possible, these kinds of problems are taken care of quickly; do not let your walls and property become a place where graffiti is acceptable for very long.

- Make certain that hallway displays and bulletin boards are changed periodically throughout the year.

- Use the building as a symbol of openness and welcome to visitors from the community.

Materials and Supplies

- Make certain that supplies ordered during the summer arrive and are distributed to staff.

- Oversee the use of consumable supplies throughout the building (e.g., chalk, paper, etc.) to make certain that there is not an interruption of material in midyear.

Communications With Staff, Students, Parents, and Community

- Work with local colleges and universities to identify appropriate placement procedures for student teachers who will be working in your building throughout the school year.

- Establish and monitor appropriate parent and community volunteer programs.

- Review standing committee structures; establish new committees where needed to carry out important work in the school.

- Plan parent meeting dates for the year with staff, PTA and PTO, and so forth.

- On a continuing basis, make certain to communicate all important dates for the year with your staff.

- Follow all established dates and procedures related to teacher and staff evaluation for the year.

- Get to know assistant principals (and other informal leaders in your building) with whom you will be working; be particularly sensitive to the need to work with any assistant principals who might have been competitors for your job.

- Develop a clear roster of staff duties and special assignments.

- Work with local colleges and universities in the placement of student teachers and interns in your building.

- Visit as many classes as time permits as often as possible.

- Review teacher lesson plans periodically, check on grading practices, and openly share with teachers your expectations regarding student performance.

- Learn the local culture of your school related to formal and informal holidays and contests. (For example, is Valentine's Day always a big day at your school? Do you have a large number of teachers and students who observe certain religious holy days each year, thus increasing the likelihood that absentee rates will be high on some dates that are not listed as official holidays on your calendar?)

System Responsibilities

- Learn the mandated census dates for your state (i.e., the official date on which enrollment must be reported to the district and state educational agency).

- Work with appropriate district personnel to learn procedures associated with establishing your building budget for the next year. (There is likely to be an absolute deadline for this material to be submitted to the central office; do not underestimate the amount of time that may be needed to carry out the task and meet deadlines.)

- Gather data systematically and continuously for the school annual report that will have to be submitted to the central office at some point toward the end of the school year. (Again, this task is much simpler and more effective if you do not wait until the last minute to gather relevant data.)

- Systematically document your personal and professional accomplishments. (This will come into play when it is time for your performance appraisal and also in the future when you may seek a different position.)

- Develop a staffing plan for the following year. This should reflect such predictable events as the retirement of some of your teachers and the need to recruit replacements.

- Make certain to meet all deadlines for the completion of important tasks such as the evaluation of untenured teachers, first-year teachers, tenured faculty, classified staff, supervision of activities and athletic programs, planning for substitute teachers, and so on. (Also comply with all stated procedures for reporting the results of the evaluation to all involved and concerned parties.)

Toward the End of the Year

A big part of every school year is the last few months and weeks when many annual events pile up, and you need to make certain that these are completed efficiently. More important, the way in which you bring about closure to one school year is often a big part of how successfully next year will start. Remember all of the things that you discovered last summer and wished that the previous principal had done before you got there? Now is the time to pretend you are going to be the person who "inherits" your work from this year, and plan accordingly.

Building Maintenance

- Work with your district facilities manager and the head custodian in your building to identify major work and improvements that need to be done after the school year has concluded (e.g., roofing, access ramps, window repairs, parking lot improvements, lighting, etc.).

- Establish a summer cleaning schedule with your building custodial staff; include minor repairs and plans for storing and securing equipment and material during the summer months.

- Carry out an inventory of instructional materials for each grade level (elementary schools) or subject department (secondary schools) used throughout the building. (For example, replace teacher manuals, overhead transparencies, duplication masters, etc., where needed.)

- Involve teachers in providing input concerning modifications that might be needed in their individual classrooms (e.g., adding window shades, bulletin boards, display boards, or lighting fixtures, and replacing damaged furniture, etc., which might be installed during the summer).

Instructional Materials

- Collect and account for textbooks and other instructional materials distributed at the beginning of the school year.

- Survey teachers to determine additional instructional materials and equipment that may be needed next year.

- Collect from teachers grade books, lesson planning books, attendance records, and other materials that may be helpful to you in talking with parents, students, and central office administrators in the absence of teachers during the summer months.

Communications With Teachers, Staff, Parents, and Students

- Get ready for end-of-the-year award ceremonies by purchasing plaques, certificates, trophies, and so forth well in advance of the dates of the ceremonies.

- Distribute a survey to parents to determine their perceptions of overall program effectiveness in the school.

- Distribute a survey to teachers to determine their perceptions of the quality of the school's program. In addition, if you are comfortable with your staff and also your sense of work as a principal, you may also wish to ask teachers to rate your performance during the past year.

- Send thank-you notes to your immediate supervisors, the district maintenance department, and others who have helped you to survive your first year.

- Order and distribute special gifts (e.g., flowers, gift certificates) to parent volunteers.

- Sponsor a special social event (breakfast, tea, etc.) for parent volunteer groups, booster clubs, and so forth.

- Send an individual, handwritten note of thanks to each teacher and staff member in your building. (Yes, even if you have a big building! A few hours of personal investment by you and a little writer's cramp will have great payoff in the future.) Be specific about the contributions that are being rewarded and appreciated.

- Inform teachers and staff members about possible summer workshops, seminars, and other professional enrichment opportunities sponsored by your district, the state department of education, the local business community, and so forth.

- Sponsor "thank-you luncheons" for your office and custodial staff.

- Submit your annual report to the central office.

- Share with staff members strategies or techniques that might be helpful in the improvement of school practices. This should be done in the spring so that staff can begin to plan for further discussion of these strategies next year.

- Alert staff to any district priorities projected for implementation next year. Again, sharing this information in the spring will make work in the fall much easier and productive.

- Lead the staff in discussions related to possible concerns that will be addressed next year. Formulate committees, encourage open dialogue during staff meetings, and plan ahead for staff inservice sessions that might be necessary next year.

General Management

- Plan the school master schedule for next year.

- Provide room assignments for next year.

- Review building policies as a way to make modifications in operations procedures for next year.

- Carry out student retention reviews for next year.

- Develop a tentative duty roster for next year.

- Review and set student activity fees for next year (and seek approval of your school board, if necessary).

- Plan and coordinate (and delegate direct responsibilities to others) such normal spring activities as the spring student play, prom, sporting events, graduation ceremonies, and so forth.

We conclude this listing of possible tasks that need to be done during different moments in your first year with two observations. First, we do not wish to suggest that our list is exhaustive or includes all that you might need to do. Undoubtedly, other important activities may be found in your situation, and some of what we have listed may never be relevant to you. The second observation is that we do not wish to suggest any particular priority here. It is not more important, for example, to send thank-you notes to the district custodial supervisor than it is to engage staff in goal setting for next year. You must make your own determination of what tasks must be done first. But it is a critical decision to make.

Building a Personal Plan

This chapter dealt with a review of many of the important technical skills that a new principal needs to master in order to become a proactive and effective leader. We suggested a large number of tasks that you may wish to carry out before the school year begins, after the year has started, and also in preparation for the closing of a school year. As you may have noted, there are a lot of things that must be accomplished, but we hope that you do not become overwhelmed with the enormous responsibilities of your job. Our goal here is to help you develop an understanding of major issues that need to be addressed in a systematic way. This type of proactive planning will assist you in becoming a true leader, not simply becoming a reactive manager of the "next crisis."

In this last section, we invite you to consider your own situation and identify some important tasks that will need to be addressed throughout the school year.

Before the year begins?

_____

_____

_____

_____

_____

_____

After the school year is under way?

_____

_____

_____

_____

_____

_____

In preparation for the end of the year?

_____

_____

_____

_____

_____

_____

Our closing thought in this chapter is that no matter how well you may plan your year, you will still encounter surprises and unplanned events, or you may discover some responsibilities for which you do not feel well prepared. In those cases, please remember that you will never be able to stand totally alone and be effective. Call other principals, seek advice from the central office, and gather input from your teachers, secretarial staff, parents, and others. After all, you can get a lot more accomplished when you work as a team.

7

Building a Personal Timeline for Learning and Development

BARBARA PHILLIPS was determined not to make the same mistakes that others made when they got their first principalships. She knew that other rookies had stepped into their jobs with the clear intention of simply "surviving" their first year by sitting back and waiting for things to happen. Barbara believed that as a new principal in a very traditional school district like Fort Grayson, she had only a brief "honeymoon period"—a window of opportunity in which she could make the kinds of changes that would enable her school to rise above the other junior high schools in the district. She was committed to "hitting the ground running" and pushing hard for reforms in her school.

At the same time, Barbara was aware of the fact that as a beginning principal, she had to learn about schools, educational administration practice, and the latest research related to effective teaching and learning. As a result, she was rapidly becoming more and more fatigued as the school year wore on. She was beginning to recognize the fact that she might be burned out before the start of the second half of the school year.

* * *

Often, when people achieve a major professional goal such as being hired as a school principal for the first time, there is an understandable tendency to want to accomplish a huge amount in as short a time as possible. Indeed, there is even some research evidence to suggest that when a person steps into a new leadership role, he or she has only about 12 to 18 months to change the organization in which he or she now works. If he or she waits too long, there is a strong tendency for the newcomer to become part of the existing scenery, part of the organization that should be changed. This finding, incidentally, is contrary to conventional wisdom that suggests that the new leader should keep a low profile when first coming on board; he or she should do nothing to upset people by trying to make too many changes too quickly. The problem, of course, is that moving too fast as a new leader has serious drawbacks. Change might occur, but the cost to the new person might be more than is reasonable as health begins to fail, personal relationships suffer, and followers get caught up in a hectic pace that cannot be maintained for very long.

As we have suggested in earlier chapters, as people have the opportunity to review their personal values, dispositions toward leadership, and actual leadership skills, we expect that they will need to develop a plan and related timeline to guide their personal and professional development as leaders. This planning process is the focus of this chapter.

One of the central themes that we want to promote throughout this book is that we do not wish simply to equip you with a collection of survival skills that you will need to get through the first year or two on the job. Of course, we realize that when you take on a new job like the principalship, you have a natural interest in learning how to increase your initial comfort by completing assigned tasks in a competent, timely, and efficient manner. We believe strongly in the often-stated belief that "you can't be a leader if you get fired!" As a result, we focus much of your attention on what you are likely to need at the start of your career. But we don't want to leave the impression that being "good enough" is truly an adequate way to look at your career as a school principal. Our persisting goal is to assist you in developing a long-term vision of leadership that goes well beyond simple survival skills.

In this chapter, we will assist you in setting up a personal guideline that you might follow as you journey from being a true "rookie" to eventual status as a veteran educational leader in your present—or some other—school system.

A Developmental Framework

Again, we start with a recognition of an important fact related to your first steps into the principalship. You want to do a good job, and the job that you have selected as a career is a big one. There may be a very strong tendency for you to want to do a lot of things right away and make certain that everything selected is a resounding success. After all, the superintendent and the school board that hired you probably told you on numerous occasions that they were pleased that you were joining them, that they had high hopes for you to "really make a difference," and that you were just the right person to do a great job! Perhaps the exact words that you heard are not what we've written here, but there is little doubt that when a new principal comes into a school, people have high hopes that the newcomer will either do the same wonderful things accomplished by his or her predecessor or make the kinds of changes that will immediately straighten up the mess left by the former principal. Slight variations on these two themes are possible, but the fact is that people want the new principal to do all sorts of important things, beginning with the first days on the job.

As a beginner, you will have a natural tendency to try to please everyone, meet all expectations, and do a truly outstanding job at all times. We will now share a major secret: You can't do all of the above. Further, if you try to do everything with equal zeal and attention right away, you are likely to be less than effective in your new job. We agree with many researchers who suggest that people proceed through clearly identifiable stages, or developmental phases, as they move into new roles. For our purposes here, we have suggested the following five phases:

Phase 1: We refer to this as "Coming on Board." This period should normally last 1 or 2 years. It begins with a person first being named to a principalship. It ends at different times for different people, but generally at that point where a person feels comfortable enough with a new role that he or she is no longer concerned about losing a job for failing to do certain assigned tasks. People who are in this phase tend to be mostly concerned with their own survival needs. As a result, discussions about long-term goals and projects for a school or district are not extremely relevant. Further, a principal in this Coming on Board phase is likely to think more about his or her own personal needs above any concerns about the professional well-being of his or her staff.

Phase 2: After a principal has developed some degree of comfort in the job, and he or she is no longer experiencing any serious anxiety about whether or not he or she is going to survive and simply do the job, that person is likely to enter a second developmental phase. After about 2 years on the job, people should start to seek new ways of measuring effectiveness and success. We call this phase the "Searching for Success" time because principals at this point in their careers realize that they can do the job, but now they wish to do the job well. This phase is a progression beyond Coming on Board, but it is still a time when principals are likely to still be more concerned with their own needs—or personal definitions of success—than they are with the broader needs of colleagues or the total school organization. On the other hand, during this time, there should be a definite shift from thinking only about survival as a reactive response to trying to move the school forward in a proactive way. Again, there is no absolute time established for this phase, but it is normally relatively brief for most people, lasting for only 1 or 2 years.

Phase 3: We call this period a time of "Looking Outward." It is at this point that many principals start to question whether what they are doing is starting to have any kind of positive effect on others. In some ways, it is very difficult to distinguish this stage from Phase 2 because during both phases principals tend to focus on the issue of impact of administrative behavior. The critical issue here, however, is that principals at this point are asking the questions, "Does what I do really have any effect on the teachers, staff, and most important, students?" and "Can I have a substantive impact on practices here so that we can improve the school?" One of the critical things to remember about this phase, if a principal enters it, is that the beginning of the phase may not happen until after 3 or 4 years of service. However, in the case of good principals, it is also a phase that will never end. We must note the fact, however, that there are some principals who spend many years in their jobs without ever achieving this phase.

Phase 4: This stage in a principal's career, which may come sometime after about 10 years on the job, may be referred to as a "Torch Passing" phase. What happens in this time is the beginning of an emphasis on trying to find, recruit, and prepare people to take an interest in moving into careers as educational leaders. This gets played out through principals taking great pride in selecting specific individuals as assistants, or by encouraging and sponsoring one or more of their teachers to think about future careers in school administration by taking courses at a local university. Principals at this developmental phase take on duties of sponsorship and, to some extent, mentorship to draw new people to the profession. It is at this point that principals often begin to take on their personal duties of developing the talents of others and improving the profession in general. Clearly, this phase is characterized largely by attention that is directed toward the needs of others, the school or district, and the profession of the principalship in general. This is a significant departure from the first two phases, in which concerns and interests are mostly inwardly directed. No defined period of time is associated with people moving into this career phase. It may occur after 5 years of being in the principalship, or after 15 or more years. In some cases, it may never be a part of an administrator's career.

Phase 5: At this point in an individual's career, there is a distinct return to personal needs and agendas. Here, attention is focused on the process of "Closing Out a Career." This might appear as getting ready for retirement, or at least some sort of shift into a career that is not the principalship. For instance, individuals get to a point where their interests are directed toward other positions such as superintendencies or other central office jobs. When a person gets to this point, he or she has more interest in other issues outside of the daily responsibilities of the principalship.

We make a few summary observations related to this listing of different developmental phases. First, these five stages are not static or linear. In other words, people might move back and forth from one phase to another. For example, an individual who moves from one principalship to another might go from Phase 3 (Looking Outward) or even Phase 4 (Torch Passing) and return to Phase 2 (Searching for Success) when faced with the prospect of learning about expectations, norms, and cultures of new schools and districts. In fact, the only phases in our model that are found at relatively predictable points in an administrative career are Phase 1 (Coming on Board) at the beginning and Phase 5 (Closing Out a Career) at the end. The second observation that we make about the five phases is that not everyone proceeds through all steps. For example, some people never become interested in Passing the Torch or even Looking Outward. They tend to remain mostly interested in their own career needs, with little concern for colleagues or even the school systems around them. Although this is unfortunate in our view, it is nevertheless a reality that people sometimes become so focused on their own situations that they forget about their professional relationships with others. It happens all the time in personal relationships. We have also seen cases where people have spent a large part of their careers in the Coming on Board phase; they never seem to learn or go beyond the limitations and perspectives of rookies. Suddenly they shift from concerns, interests, and behaviors associated with newcomers to think about Closing Out a Career. These principals literally go through an entire career without getting out of the starting block. We doubt that people intend to do this, but it is a pattern that can happen if one focuses too early and too exclusively on simply surviving as a principal.

One final observation that we make about the phases is that none of these steps is bounded by any strict time limits. For example, we have seen people proceed quickly through the first three phases, often within the first 2 or 3 years of their professional lives. Then they spend the majority of their careers consciously serving as mentors to other practicing or aspiring educational administrators. We have also seen cases where people have moved rapidly to the Closing Out a Career stage because the major goal they had in becoming a principal in the first place was to use it as a stepping stone on their way to the superintendency, a higher education position, or some other job in education.

We assume that you can think of examples of individual principals who were in one or another of the phases we have noted in this chapter. You may wish to sit down and list some examples of things that you have already encountered at one or more of the phases that we have identified:

_____

_____

————————————————————————————————————

————————————————————————————————————

————————————————————————————————————

————————————————————————————————————

What's This Got to Do With Me?

Although these phases may be of interest to those concerned with looking at and analyzing the long-term career paths of school administrators, what relevance do they have for someone like you, who is either getting ready to step into a principalship for the first time or going through the first year or two on the job? After all, does it make any sense to think about serving as a mentor someday in the future when you are still trying to find a colleague to help you now?

Frankly, we believe that unless you realize and look at how careers progress in total, you may be frustrated and limited as you start your life as a principal. Typically, individuals walk into school systems where their colleague principals are distributed across all of these phases, with one exception. It is not unusual for a person to be the only principal who is Coming on Board at a single time. As a result, a person can get lost in an environment where everyone else is either thinking about retirement or at least focused almost exclusively on Searching for Success as a personal concern. Although we strongly suggest (as you will see in a later chapter) that any newly hired principal needs to find a mentor, the fact is that some districts have no principals who are even remotely interested in Torch Passing. Although we will talk later about the issue of finding mentors, we suggest here that when a district has no one to serve as a mentor, it may be necessary for a new principal to seek support from an administrator in another school system.

Another implication from the phases that relates to the needs of a beginning principal is the fact that knowing about this predictable progression that may take place in a career might help you in thinking about your life as an administrator "down the road." For example, we think that it is important for you to recognize that it is understandable that the first few years on the job you might spend a lot of your time and energy thinking about personal needs. This is important. We have seen numerous cases where rookie principals have expressed anxiety and almost a sense of guilt over the fact that they were not accomplishing as much as they wanted to accomplish as quickly as they had hoped. They were not becoming the effective instructional leaders suggested as goals in the research literature. Instead, they felt as if most of their time was being invested in personal concerns. The first few years are likely to be ones in which individuals establish their own sense of identity and comfort in their roles. As one new principal once told us, "I can't get too concerned about changing the world until I get my own house in order first." It is perfectly understandable that you are probably not getting too involved with thoughts of Torch Passing just yet. On the other hand, there is a temptation to begin to feel guilty about not getting involved with more than personal interests. After all, in many cases, new principals are alone as rookies in their school systems. As a result, it is not unusual for the newcomer to feel apart from colleagues, and not necessarily completely committed to the goals and objectives of the larger school system. As more than one beginning principal has told us over the years, "Before I become a great instructional leader, I just want to get through each day of my first year on the job!"

Each new principal will need to establish his or her own realistic timeline that will permit movement from one phase of development to another. Some people will be able to move very quickly during the first few weeks of service from simply Coming on Board to a situation where they are already looking for ways of improving the overall programs for teachers, students, parents, and the whole community. This might be based on a whole variety of reasons, such as the nature of their teaching staffs, the size of the district, the quality of their preservice preparation program (and internship experiences), whether or not they have an assistant principal, whether they worked in this district before as a teacher, and so forth. Some people may need more than a year to go beyond initial culture shock and progress beyond the Coming on Board phase. The important thing that any new principal needs to remember is that time spent as a rookie is valuable time in terms of a long-term career. Don't rush too quickly toward trying to learn a whole new system and change the world in 1 month, simply because the "research" on effective schools says that principals must make an immediate difference. It simply is not going to happen overnight for everyone. And you should not get discouraged if you don't understand everything as quickly as you had hoped that you might.

The key to effectiveness is not going too fast or dragging your feet waiting for the "perfect" time to foster change. Perhaps a very effective strategy to follow is the development of a realistic set of annual plans to guide your work each year. This is an organized way to initiate change, while also allowing you to look at the nature of your school in a clear fashion. This type of planning might begin during your second year as a principal, and it probably ought to continue throughout your career. In the next section, an outline for this type of systematic planning is provided.

Developing a Personal Timeline for Action

A critical part of preparing a personal professional development portfolio and action plan involves not only stating *what* you plan to do, but even more important, *when* you are going to do things. In this last section of this chapter, we propose that you develop a personal timeline that you will follow as you set out to meet certain important professional goals during your first year on the job. Remember, you simply cannot accomplish everything at once, but you may never accomplish anything without a serious plan to determine which things are to happen first. Another helpful tip might be to make certain that you bounce these goals off a few people whom you trust. This type of feedback can be very useful to you in thinking about goals and priorities.

GOAL I

The first thing I hope to accomplish in this first year as a new principal is:

_____

_____

I hope to achieve this goal by:

_____

_____

The latest date that I would expect to be able to achieve this goal is:

_____

_____

GOAL II

The second goal that I hope to accomplish this year is:

_____

_____

I hope to achieve this goal by:

_____

_____

The latest date that I would expect to achieve this goal is:

_____

_____

GOAL III

The third goal that I hope to achieve this year is:

_____

_____

I hope to achieve this goal by:

_____

_____

The latest date that I would expect to achieve this goal is:

_____

_____

The fact that we conclude this section by providing a place for you to write three goals is not meant to suggest that as a first-year principal you shouldn't try more than three things. At the same time, we don't want to signal a belief that you should try too many things. The ultimate answer to the question of what is the right number of things for a rookie to try is something that only you can provide. How much is enough, and which things should be done first, is not something that we can prescribe in this book. Nor is it something that your superintendents, school board, or central office can dictate. It is legitimate, of course, for superintendents to charge principals with goals that need to be addressed in all schools of the district. After all, you are part of a larger system. However, if your personal objective is simply to make certain that you do not do anything contrary to what your bosses tell you to do, then you will do little more than follow their priorities as much as possible. On the other hand, what you do, when you do it, and how you do it will always be matters that come from within you and your individual set of values and beliefs. Once again, the platform exercise that we described earlier is critical to your success. And sharing that platform with others—your staff as well as the superintendent—will do much to increase effective communication so that you can meet the expectations of others and also focus on your personal objectives with equal commitment.

8

Others' Expectations

WHEN FRANK LUJAN accepted his current position as the principal of the Graystone Elementary School, he felt a mixture of both confidence and anxiety to an extent he had never quite felt before in his professional life. He believed that he had enough experience as a teacher to appreciate some of the major issues that needed to be addressed in an effective elementary school. He also had learned enough in the traditional administrative task areas of law, finance, supervision, and personnel when he completed his graduate work at State University.

On the other hand, Frank was not totally comfortable with the expectations that others had for his performance. He knew that he wanted to spend a lot of time working with teachers to assist them in improving their efforts to help the kids. That seemed to be a statement that made a lot of sense to those who talked with him during the three interviews that preceded his getting this job. However, last week, when the superintendent met with the new principals, Frank heard a somewhat different message about getting the year off to a good start by taking charge of things through sharing personal visions and goals with the teachers and staff. Back at State University, Frank's adviser and mentor, Dr. Norman Galloway, always told him that his most critical job as a beginning principal was to make certain that "the chalk was in the classrooms and the light bulbs were illuminating the thinking in the school." That was Dr. Galloway's approach to letting Frank know that he had to make certain that the technical and managerial details of the principal's job were very important.

Frank was truly looking forward to his new life as a school principal but in fact, he was more than a bit confused about whose voice he should be hearing now that the school year was about to get underway.

* * *

Frank Lujan is not the only beginning principal who has been given so much "good advice" that he did not get any good advice at all. The fact is, just about everyone has a different idea about what you should be doing now that you are in charge. In the long run, you will have to make your own decisions as to what should be done, and how you should define your job as a principal. But it is critical to note that there are likely to be numerous competing definitions and descriptions of what you should be doing.

In this chapter, we tackle the issue of competing expectations of what you are supposed to do now that you are a principal. We will present research findings about what different individuals such as superintendents, experienced principals, and aspiring principals have to say about the most important aspects of your job. In the long run, you will have to be the person who decides what is most critical about your work, but we share here some alternative perspectives that may be of some interest to you.

Critical Skills for Beginning Principals: A Survey

Before going any further with our discussion of the kinds of skills that different groups expect of you as a beginning principal, we suggest that you take a moment to respond to the items on the survey in Figure 8.1, the Beginning Principals' Critical Skills Inventory. We developed this instrument a few years ago to do the research that serves as the basis for this chapter.

Scale I (Items 1-8) deals with items that are associated with the technical and managerial duties of principals. These tend to be the kinds of job responsibilities that are found in job descriptions or policy manuals of school districts. Scale II (Items 9-16) deals with issues that are defined as socialization skills, or things that a person needs to know, do, or demonstrate in order to fit into a new organization. Finally, Scale III (Items 17-24) is composed of items that are self-awareness skills, or items that touch on one's personal ability to know one's own values, attitudes, and beliefs as they are related to a professional role.

Now that you've had a chance to complete the Beginning Principals' Critical Skills Inventory yourself, you have rank-ordered the three broad categories of Technical and Managerial Skills (Scale I), Socialization Skills (Scale II), and Self-Awareness Skills (Scale III). In the next section of this chapter, we will look at your ratings as they compare with those of other individuals who also participated in this research over the past few years. We believe that you will soon appreciate the fact that even among professional school administrators, there is little absolute consensus as to the "ideal" duties of principals.

Directions: For each of the following duties assigned to principals, please assess the extent to which each item is critical to your ability to do your job. Use the following scale in responding to each item:

> 5 = *Extremely important*
> 4 = *Somewhat important*
> 3 = *Neutral* (not extremely important or totally unimportant)
> 2 = *Somewhat unimportant*
> 1 = *Totally unimportant*

Scale (Circle One) Item

Scale (Circle One)	Item
5 4 3 2 1	1. How to evaluate staff (i.e., procedures for the task and also the substance: What do standards really mean?)
5 4 3 2 1	2. How to facilitate/conduct group meetings
5 4 3 2 1	3. How to design and implement a data-based improvement process, including goal-setting and evaluation
5 4 3 2 1	4. How to develop and monitor a building budget
5 4 3 2 1	5. How to organize and conduct parent-teacher-student conferences
5 4 3 2 1	6. How to establish a scheduling program (master schedule) for students and staff
5 4 3 2 1	7. Awareness of issues related to local school law
5 4 3 2 1	8. How to manage food service, custodial, and secretarial staff
5 4 3 2 1	9. Establishing a positive and cooperative relationship with other district administrators
5 4 3 2 1	10. How to determine who is what in a school setting
5 4 3 2 1	11. Knowing how to relate to school board members and central office personnel
5 4 3 2 1	12. Knowing where the limits exist with the district or building and balancing that knowledge with one's own professional values
5 4 3 2 1	13. Understanding how the principalship changes family and other personal relationships
5 4 3 2 1	14. Developing interpersonal networking skills that may be used with individuals inside and outside of the system

Figure 8.1. The Beginning Principals' Critical Skills Inventory

Scale (Circle One)	Item

5 4 3 2 1   15. Ability to encourage involvement by all parties in the educational system

5 4 3 2 1   16. How to develop positive relationships with other organizations and agencies located in the school's surrounding community

5 4 3 2 1   17. Demonstrating an awareness of what it means to possess organizational power and authority

5 4 3 2 1   18. Demonstrating an awareness of why one was selected for a leadership position in the first place

5 4 3 2 1   19. Portraying a sense of self-confidence on the job

5 4 3 2 1   20. Having a vision along with an understanding needed to achieve organizational goals

5 4 3 2 1   21. Demonstrating a desire to make a significant difference in the lives of students

5 4 3 2 1   22. Being aware of one's biases, strengths, and weaknesses

5 4 3 2 1   23. Understanding and seeing that change is ongoing and that it results in a continually changing vision of the principalship

5 4 3 2 1   24. How to assess job responsibilities in terms of the "real role" of the principal

Scoring: Now add up your scores in the following ways:

Scale I: Items 1–8 = _____ divided by 8 = _____

Scale II: Items 9–16 = _____ divided by 8 = _____

Scale III: Items 17–24 = _____ divided by 8 = _____

Rank-order your three average scores per scale:

_____

_____

_____

Figure 8.1. The Beginning Principals' Critical Skills Inventory (Continued)

Other Beginners

If you rank-ordered the three skill areas from most to least important, as follows:

1. Technical and Managerial Skills
2. Socialization Skills
3. Self-Awareness Skills

you were in line with the majority of other beginners (i.e., principals in their 1st, 2nd, or 3rd years on the job), who also participated in this research. In addition, you were consistent with a high percentage of aspiring principals (people currently enrolled in university preservice preparation programs leading to state certification or licensure).

Of all 24 items on the survey, which one did you believe to be the single most important one?

_____

_____

Which was the least important single item?

_____

_____

In our research, we have found that people who were enrolled in training programs leading to certification as principals or beginning principals rated Item 7, "Awareness of issues related to local school law," as the most critical skill to be demonstrated by principals, whereas Item 17, "Demonstrating an awareness of what it means to possess organizational power and authority," was viewed as least important skill.

What might these responses imply to you, in terms of the perceptions held by colleagues who are not yet in the principalship or who have also recently stepped into their first administrative assignments?

_____

_____

_____

_____

_____

_____

Experienced Principals

Of the 24 items on the Beginning Principals' Critical Skills Inventory, which do you believe were rated as most important by principals with at least 3 years of experience?

_____

_____

Which items from the survey were probably rated as least important by the experienced principals, in your mind?

_____

_____

According to the principals who responded to this research, the most critical skill to be demonstrated by a beginning principal was Item 10, "How to determine who is what in a school setting." This item was followed closely by Item 9, "Establishing a positive and cooperative relationship with other district administrators." Both of these items were in the cluster related to Socialization Skills.

According to practicing principals, the least relevant items that need to be demonstrated by beginning colleagues were items such as "How to manage food service, custodial, and secretarial staff" (Item 8), and "How to establish a scheduling program (master schedule) for students and staff" (Item 6). These items, and most others that were among the lowest-ranked issues, were clustered in the Technical and Managerial Skills category.

What are some of the reasons why you believe that experienced principals might rank the above items as they did?

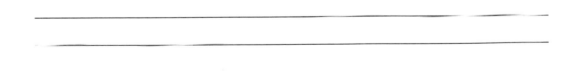

Superintendents

The last group of educators that responded to this survey were superintendents who had hired new principals in their school districts during the last 3 years. Their reasons followed very different patterns from those of beginning and aspiring principals, and also from those of beginning principals. What items do you believe that superintendents viewed as most critical for beginning principals?

_____

_____

What do superintendents view as the least important skills that need to be
exhibited by beginning building administrators?

_____

_____

Of all the skills listed in the Beginning Principals' Critical Skills Inventory, the
one indicated as most important by superintendents who had experience with
hiring and working with new principals in recent years was Item 18, "Demonstrating an awareness of why one was selected for a leadership position in the first
place." Second on the list of priorities valued by superintendents was Item 19,
"Portraying a sense of self-confidence on the job."

The lowest items on the superintendents' list were Item 8, "How to manage
food service, custodial, and secretarial staff," and Item 6, "How to establish a
scheduling program (master schedule) for students and staff."

In terms of the broad categories of skills measured through the survey, Table
8.1 shows how the priorities of the three groups surveyed look when compared.

So What Does This Mean?

The fact that different groups hold different expectations for what school
principals are supposed to do is not a new or astonishing finding. However, the
study reported here has provided some important insights into differences that,
in turn, are related to finding more effective ways of guiding people through personal career transitions, and also providing people with more successful experiences as beginning school principals.

The implications of our research on perceptions related to critical skills for
beginning principals are clear in the area of induction programs designed to assist
novice school administrators. For example, we believe that the findings of this
study that suggest that experienced principals and superintendents value colleagues' abilities to demonstrate greater self-confidence and ability to "fit" into the
social context of a school district constitute a great argument in favor of adopting
mentoring schemes for new principals. In Chapter 10, we will return to this topic
in some additional detail. However, we note here that mentoring for new principals is often missing the mark with regard to the real issues facing beginners. The
majority of mentoring programs we have reviewed have tended to focus on helping people to learn critical technical and managerial skills associated with work in
a particular school system. We are not suggesting that such skills are unimportant,
or that beginners always have an immediate grasp of how to do a number of specific things. On the other hand, it may be considerably more important for a dis-

TABLE 8.1 Skills Priority Comparison for School Administrators

	Beginning Principals' Ranking	Practicing Principals' Ranking	Superintendents' Ranking
Technical and Managerial Skills	1	3	3
Socialization Skills	2	1	2
Self-Awareness Skills	3	2	1

trict wanting to support novice principals to invest scarce professional development resources in a program addressing issues that typically could be handled by assigning experienced secretaries to beginners, or by inviting people to call the central office with any questions about local operating procedures.

Mentoring for beginning principals is a desirable practice. However, such a practice works best if it is directed largely at supporting first-year administrators in their efforts to increase their skill levels in the areas related to increased socialization and self-awareness to the job and to a new system. Such mentoring ideally focuses on the needs and feelings of the individual as he or she proceeds during the first year or two of service as an administrator.

We do not wish to suggest that the establishment of mentoring relationships will automatically guide you through a successful first year. Having a mentor will certainly help, but there are things that you can do as an individual as well. Understanding that different groups of people have different expectations regarding what you are supposed to do is extremely important. Our research noted that you probably believe that the most critical tasks for principals to perform are to take care of the technical and managerial side of your job—maintain the budget and schedule, keep within the law, and so forth. These are certainly important things for any principal to do. However, it is important to note that your colleagues will expect other behaviors. Other principals in your district want good colleagues—people who fit in with them and contribute to the well-being of the school district in general. Superintendents want people who are confident—who believe that they can do the job for which they were hired. In short, the research findings here suggest that you will not be viewed by others as very successful if you spend all of your time "taking care of business" in your school. Others expect that you can do the job according to the district's published job description. They want you to add your own personality and ability to the quality of life in your new "home." That may be one of the reasons why a lot of beginning principals are shocked to find out that they are not evaluated highly by their own school systems, even when they have spent a lot of time in their own buildings doing the job that they believe they were hired to do!

One additional word of explanation and, perhaps, caution. Although our research found that there are differences in how various groups look at the relative importance of skills that need to be demonstrated by beginning principals, we did not find that any of the individual items or categories of skills (technical and managerial, socialization, or self-awareness) was totally unimportant. Every item on the survey was viewed as critical. All that we have discovered is that when faced with the need to prioritize, different groups find certain items more important than others. Although the information presented here is meant to guide you and give you some notion of how others might look at your job, we wish to emphasize that in large measure, how you personally view your job and its various responsibilities and tasks must be a matter for you to define on your own. Once again, we emphasize the importance of understanding and remaining consistent with your own personal and professional platform as a way to guide decisions in this area.

Your Personal Plan

We conclude the chapter by asking you to make plans to incorporate the concepts learned in this chapter within your personal professional portfolio as a way to guide your growth as a principal. Now that we have had the opportunity to think about the kinds of skills that you value, as seen through your responses to the Beginning Principals' Critical Skills Inventory, as compared with the perceptions of others, where do you believe there is the greatest degree of difference between what you value and what experienced principals and superintendents value?

_____

_____

_____

_____

_____

_____

In what areas do you find the greatest similarities and overlaps between your assumptions about critical skills and the assumptions of experienced principals and superintendents?

_____

_____

_____

_____

_____

_____

In the space below, note some of the ways in which you plan to address the differences that exist between your perceptions of critical skills and the perceptions of your colleagues.

_____

_____

_____

_____

_____

_____

9

Reading the Signs in a System

MICHAEL DANDRIDGE was extremely excited on this, his first day as the new principal of Rhinegold Middle School. Although he had 3 years of experience as a junior high school assistant principal in another nearby community, he had always looked forward to the day when he would have his own building. He had always wanted to step into a setting where he could have a chance to implement some of the ideas he had concerning more effective ways to help early adolescents. Michael had been very successful as a middle school teacher for several years. He enjoyed a reputation as a very innovative teacher. It was not surprising that he now saw a chance of carrying out a lot of his dreams through his new role as the leader of a school. He would be the instructional leader of Rhinegold.

Michael was thinking about the kinds of things he wanted to do to change the school's curriculum and instructional practices as he walked into his office for the first time in July. Of course, he had been in the school before, when he came for the interview, and also when the superintendent took him for a "walk-through" the day after the school board approved his appointment. But on both occasions, he looked, but he really didn't see much. He was so excited about the things he planned to do as the new principal that he really couldn't recall many of the details of his new school's physical environment. It was a bit like the experience that he and his wife had many years ago when they bought their first home. A few hours after they signed an offer to buy the house, they knew very little about the details of what they had just purchased. All they knew was that it was their home, and they were happy. Ill-fitting doors and cracks on the basement floor were hidden by their immediate enthusiasm.

Michael looked around his new office at Rhinegold and noticed that it was a large enough room with a nice pair of windows that looked out on the playground of the school. He also realized that the room was extremely hot—a fact that he didn't recognize when he came through the building last spring when it was still rather cold outside, or when the superintendent took him through the building late last Tuesday evening. There was an air conditioner installed by the last principal, but Michael didn't plan to use it much. He really didn't mind the heat. After all, he didn't intend to spend that much time in his office anyway. And besides that, this was his school!

Michael also noted two additional features of his office that he hadn't really paid much attention to before taking the keys. First, there was a large bookcase covering one wall. It was filled with books and manuals left by the previous principal who hadn't been back to collect a lot of his personal belongings since transferring to another middle school in the district. Michael looked at the titles of the materials left on the shelves. In addition to the expected items such as the district policy manual and the district curriculum guides, all the other reading material dealt with either classroom management techniques or approaches to student discipline.

The thing that concerned Michael much more was the presence of two study carrels facing another wall in the office. When Michael asked the secretary why these were being stored in the principal's office, she smiled and said that they weren't being stored there; they were part of the furnishings that had been there as long as the previous principal had been at Rhinegold. Those study carrels were being used in the in-school suspension program. The principal personally supervised students placed on "ISS," as it was called in this district.

Michael made a mental note to box up the books and call the former principal that afternoon. The custodian had already moved the carrels out into the hallway so that they could be taken to the central office warehouse for storage. After all, Michael didn't plan on being the in-school suspension monitor. He was going to be an instructional leader, not a cop!

*   *   *

Start out by describing the principal of Rhinegold before Michael Dandridge came on board.

_____

_____

_____

_____

_____

_____

Some of the descriptors that emerge about Michael's predecessor include "strictness," "attentive to discipline," "unwillingness to go out of his office very much," and "uninvolved with instructional practices." These might be unfair generalizations concerning a person's entire professional career or presence in a particular school. However, the carrels for student discipline, the nature of the books, and the fact that the principal's office was air-conditioned contribute to an image of what the former building administrator did. It doesn't mean that what took place in the past was necessarily bad. The fact that the previous principal was in his role at Rhinegold for several years probably means that the way in which he approached his job was viewed by many as quite effective.

This points to an important issue that a new principal needs to address, namely, how to reconcile his or her new ways of approaching the principalship with those of the last principal. It is important for the newcomer to ask, "What did the staff expect of the last principal?" as a way to understand what they now expect. In the case of Michael Dandridge at Rhinegold Middle School, what are likely to be some of the expectations that the staff has of a principal who steps in to follow the person who had the carrels in his office?

Once again, it is impossible to say absolutely what teachers at Rhinegold had as images of the role of the principal. But we suspect that a lot of people may have thought that the last person was good because he took care of the "bad boys and girls" so that the teachers wouldn't be bothered with that type of problem. The former principal appears to have been a person who didn't spend much of his time out in the school, in teachers' classes, or otherwise "bothering the staff." Instead, the principal of the last few years stayed in his office and responded to the needs of his teachers by making certain that the school was calm, orderly, and well disciplined. Teachers could teach effectively because the principal took care of all the trouble. And the principal appeared comfortable in that role. After all, his professional library reflected a serious interest in learning about student discipline and behavior management.

Michael Dandridge may be in for quite a shock when his teachers return from their summer vacation and find the study carrels gone from the principal's office and the principal out in the halls, visiting classrooms and observing teachers. "How will the new guy ever be able to do what Mr. X used to do?" will be a frequent question heard in the faculty lounge. The next few weeks, or even months, will represent a very difficult transition period wherein teachers will need to recognize that the old principal is gone and, more importantly, so is the old image of what a principal is supposed to do to help teachers. Michael could be in for a tough time if he does not appreciate these subtle but critical issues. We do not advocate trying to maintain the old system and image for no reason other than to make teachers comfortable. Quite the contrary, we realize that change is often needed and that the new principal has been hired largely to bring about that kind of change. But it is critical that a newcomer realize what existed in the past, celebrate that history, and then move slowly and cautiously into the future.

Don't Just Look . . . See

The school you have just inherited has a lot of important signs that you need to be able to see if you are going to understand the culture, appreciate it, celebrate it, and then move on. Michael Dandridge could have been in for a terrible first year if he had looked at the book titles and study carrels and had not *seen* what they truly represented. On one hand, what was present was a lot of clutter in a small office and some other principal's books. Taking time to see might enable a principal like Michael to appreciate a lot of culture, history, symbols, and in general, values and expectations of a community.

What did you know about the culture of the school where you now work prior to coming to work there for the first time? (Note: If you are working as the principal of a school in which you used to serve as a teacher or in some other capacity, is your view of the school now what it was in the past? Why or why not?)

_____

_____

_____

_____

List some of the things that you saw when you first came to your present school and that interested you as signs of "the way they do things around here."

_____

_____

_____

_____

What did you do in response to the things that you saw?

_____

_____

_____

_____

When a newcomer first arrives, or even a person who is supposedly familiar with a place but from a different perspective, it is critical that that person spend time looking very carefully at the whole environment as a way to see what kind of story is told. For example, did the former principal arrange his or her desk in a way that it served as a kind of barrier to people who came into the office? Are the classrooms reflective of a lot of informal teaching settings for small-group discussions, or does it appear that the preferred mode of instruction in the school centered around very formal, lecture-style classroom arrangements? If so, what might these signs suggest about the climate or "feel" of the school in which you now work? What do you see in the teachers' rooms? Is there evidence of a lot of kidding around or joking that seems to be part of the ways in which teachers interact? If you see your office decorated with your predecessor's belongings, are there any examples of teachers' relationships with "the boss"? For example, are there such things as "gag gifts," cartoon clips, or memory books provided by the staff?

The critical issue that we wish to underline here is that "a school is not a school is not a school is not . . . " Each building, regardless of size, location, level of students served, geographic site, and just about any other variable selected has a completely different reality, history, and "feel" about it. Like individual people, schools have different personalities and profiles that must be appreciated. Often, these characteristics are easier to identify than one might assume. If the newcomer takes time to see the subtle signs of the system, rather than simply looking things over, the true reality of a school will generally be apparent. Don't forget, too, that you need to be able to identify the nature of what many call the "informal organization" of your school. Here, we are talking about the people and things that don't have formal titles but influence what goes on in your school each day. Informal leaders of your school, or key influentials, need to be recognized as soon as possible.

Listen . . . Don't Just Hear

What we have noted about the importance of seeing a school and not simply looking at it is similar to our recommendation concerning the need to take time to listen to what is happening in a school. It is important to remain attentive to the sounds and language of your new environment. These things also provide many subtle indications of the climate and informal organization in which you now work.

Listen carefully to the words that teachers use to describe the students. Are they indicative of a feeling of warmth and support? Or is there an indication of some kind of constant battling between "us" and "them"? Do the "war stories" shared in the teachers' lounge reflect instances of adults controlling kids ("You should have seen how I got those kids to shape up last period!"), or are the stories shared about successes in achieving positive results ("My third-period English class was really great this morning. You should have seen the presentations they made!")? Of course, most schools will have a mixture of both kinds of teacher talk about their work with students. But in some schools we have visited, there is a definite sense that a prevailing "philosophy" of the teachers relative to their work with students is visible and needs to be recognized (if not necessarily endorsed) by a new principal. One of the challenges that a principal may face involves changing staff attitudes toward children. But changes cannot take place on the first day, and ignoring past attitudes will not help the change process.

How would you describe the "teacher talk" about students and other issues in your school?

_____

_____

_____

_____

Another important indicator of your new school is the things that you hear in your office, as secretaries, aides, custodians, nurses, cafeteria workers, or other staff members make contact with parents, students, teachers, and members of the general public. Again, we suggest that any new principal would do well to listen attentively to the tone of language (friendly and cordial, or too businesslike and cold?) that people use with individuals from outside the school. Have you ever called a business on the phone and then decided to go somewhere else simply because of the way you were addressed? People experience the same feelings when they call a school. If you knew nothing about your school other than the sound of your secretary's voice, what impressions would you have of your building?

_____

_____

_____

_____

Another thing that listening to subtle sounds in your school will tell you is the degree of formality that exists in the building in which you have recently become the principal. Do teachers call you by your first name immediately, or do they tend to refer to you more formally? How do they refer to each other? It is not surprising to hear teachers who have worked with each other for years continue to use formal terms in addressing each other ("Mr. Jones" or "Mrs. Smith"), at least during the course of the school day, and particularly in big-city schools. This may surprise you, but respect it. Some practices will never die; calling Mrs. Johnson "Sara" in front of her students may be offensive and may lead to a distance between you and a teacher who might otherwise be one of your strongest supporters.

Walk through the halls of your school and listen attentively to the sounds that you hear, the sounds coming out of teachers' classrooms. Is there a lot of good-natured laughing, or a considerable amount of raised voices, indicating teachers disciplining students? Or is it extremely quiet? Any of these signs may be indicative of the general tone of your school. If a person who knew little about your school walked through the halls and listened, what kind of impression would he or she take away after a day?

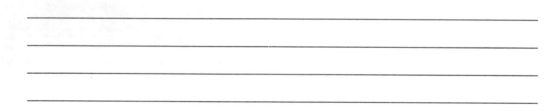

Celebrate the Past

There is a natural, unavoidable contradiction when a new principal walks into a school. On one hand, there is great expectation that the new leader will do something different, bring about change of some sort, and in general, make some kind of difference. This is true whether the former principal was viewed as extremely positive or as ineffective. People expect a newcomer to represent a new order of things. On the other hand, schools are fragile and normally very conservative organizations. "The way we've always done things" is a pretty strong value that people seek to maintain. Thus the new principal might be criticized for not doing enough and also doing too much at the same time.

If we return to the case that started this chapter, consider the dilemma facing Michael Dandridge. He knew that the district hired him to serve as an instructional leader, but he noticed that his predecessor had been primarily an office-bound disciplinarian. If he didn't bring about change and assert himself in one way, he would get in trouble with the central office and school board. On the other hand, when he threw out the carrels and made a statement that he would no longer take on student discipline as his primary duty, his teachers would be upset. What was he to do?

The principal upon whom we patterned our fictional Michael Dandridge is now in his fifth year at "Rhinegold Middle School," and is respected by his teachers and the central office as well. However, if we could invent a magic instrument called a "retrospectroscope" to allow us to look backward we could second-guess things that made his beginning as a principal more difficult than it had to be.

Perhaps the most significant thing that Michael did that may have made his arrival at his new school a bit more troublesome was the fact that he did not talk to any of his staff members about their perceptions as to why the former principal did some of the things that he did. We are not suggesting that Michael did not have the right to try to change the image of the principalship from one of chief disciplinarian to instructional leader. In fact, we commend his efforts in that regard. But when he simply took steps to remove any sign of his predecessor from the school, he was symbolically denying something that many of his teachers probably did not feel comfortable about losing. Even if many of the teachers did not truly like the former principal, Michael's actions seemed to suggest that the principal and the teachers were wrong last year. At the very least, we think that it was important for Michael to share what he planned to do with several teachers. He could have assured them that his actions were not meant to discredit the fine work of the past. Rather, he was simply trying to start things off with a different perspective of "the new kid on the block."

Another thing that Michael could have done shortly after the beginning of the new school year was to invite the former principal to drop by to visit his old school and see how Michael had decorated his old office and, in general, make a public statement about how the former principal was still valued as an important part of the "Rhinegold Team."

Do you have any additional suggestions as to how the shift from one principal to the next could have been made a bit less traumatic?

_____

_____

_____

_____

It is critical that new principals do not charge into their new settings so forcefully that they do not give honor to the past. Former staff members, practices, policies, and traditions might need to be replaced, but they need to be publicly respected because they represent so many subtle aspects of life in an organization. Any newly arrived administrator who does not celebrate the good work of the past will face many unnecessary battles with people who might see the newcomer as unfeeling or insensitive to the local culture. By the same token, remember that one of the things that a new leader needs to do is assess the practices of the past and determine things that were done before but were viewed negatively by teachers, parents, and others. Simply wanting to avoid the appearance of getting rid of all past practice does not mean that you must be bound to repeat undesirable work as well.

Developing an Action Plan

Describe the most important aspects of the school culture that you have inherited as the new principal, that is, the kinds of things that must be understood as you step in as the new leader.

_____

_____

_____

_____

_____

Which elements of the past culture represent things with which you cannot live comfortably as the new principal?

_____

_____

_____

_____

_____

What practices appear to have been least popular with faculty, students, or parents?

_____

_____

_____

_____

_____

How do you plan to step away from those past practices in a way that will not alienate you from your staff or other important people in your school environment?

_____

_____

_____

_____

_____

In what ways do you hope to replace the things with which you are not comfortable in your new school? Why?

_____

_____

_____

_____

_____

What are some of the features of your new school that you believe should be maintained as much as possible? Why?

_____

_____

_____

_____

_____

10

Building a Support System

TONI SPENCER had just suffered through what was undoubtedly the single worst day of her first year as an elementary school principal. Before she had even left her house this morning, she got a call from Harriet Wilson, her secretary (and virtual assistant principal) who said that she had a family emergency and would not be in today and perhaps the remainder of the week. When Toni arrived at school, she found Hank Gentry, her custodian, busily trying to scrub some fresh graffiti off one of the doors to the playground. Next, while Toni was working with the substitute secretary (a woman who made it clear that she would probably not like to work for long in an elementary school) to orient her to the front office routine of the day, the phone rang almost endlessly. In less than 5 minutes, Toni received word that two teachers were going to be late, and three more were ill and would not be in at all today. Substitutes would be needed today. That was fine, except Toni knew that subs were really hard to find this week. The neighboring Mountain City Schools were in the midst of a lengthy teachers' strike, and their school board was bound and determined to keep the schools open by bringing in substitutes from every suburban school district around. And that meant that Toni would not have a lot of luck in finding subs at the last minute. This was going to be one of those days when "creative class coverage" would take effect. Toni knew she would be in a classroom most of the morning.

Taking over classes from time to time was not something that Toni did not like. In fact, she looked forward to getting "back in the trenches" to work with the kids from time to time. But today, she knew that the President of her PTO would be visiting the school just before lunch to talk about the big spring fashion luncheon. And Dr. Crawford, the district director of evaluation, needed to talk to her about the testing schedule for the primary grades. That had to be done today; the school board committee on testing was meeting for dinner this evening.

Despite all the things that were on her mind, Toni had the day pretty well under control by midmorning, and she felt as if this tough day was on the "down side," and that it would be over before it got any worse. She was just returning to her office from one of the fourth-grade rooms where a substitute couldn't find a class roster when Mrs. Turner, the substitute secretary, met her in the hall to tell her about a sixth-grade student who had just been brought down to her office by the phys. ed. teacher for carrying a knife into class. She also heard that the fire department was likely to pull a fake fire alarm at some point today and that the superintendent was coming over later with a parent but that "he didn't want to discuss the issue over the phone." Toni was also still in some degree of shock over a conversation that she had had a few minutes ago with a group of sixth-grade boys who told her that they had seen a fifth grader passing out what they thought were drugs on a vacant lot a few blocks from school earlier this morning.

It was another one of those days when "lunch" (two candy bars and a cup of instant coffee) didn't come until nearly 2:00. As soon as Toni was able to get to her office for a few minutes to reflect on her discussion with the superintendent and the irate parent, the fire alarm, the in-school suspension given to the sixth-grade "knife" (actually, can opener) carrier, and about a dozen other situations that had arisen that day, the phone rang. An officer from the police department was calling to alert her that she might be visited by a man claiming to be the father of one of her third graders. This same person—a known child molester—had appeared at other elementary schools in another suburb a few times over the past 2 weeks. If he did show up, Toni was advised to keep an eye on him, try to divert him from the children, and call the police immediately, all without doing anything to tip off the unwanted visitor before the police could arrive. The first thing that Toni did after getting off the phone was visit each of her teachers and quietly explain the situation so that they would be aware of the potential problem.

Now, it was nearly 5:00. Toni had already gotten word that her secretary would be out for the entire week, the substitute secretary didn't like how cold the office was, two of today's absent teachers would be out again tomorrow, and three more teachers were going to a district workshop on inclusion tomorrow. Toni faced having at least five teachers out tomorrow, an unhappy secretary (who might not even report to work), and the consequences of a number of disciplinary decisions that she had had to make, including the in-school suspension. Angry parents were sure to be in her office tomorrow. But that would be after Toni got to work a bit late because she would park down the street from the vacant lot where the drug dealing was supposedly taking place. She hadn't completely believed the story she heard yesterday, but she didn't want to discount the tale either. She wanted to see things with her own eyes before she called the police. And the "impostor father" might show up at any time. In addition, Toni was worried about her own children—one of whom was a third-grade girl at another school in the district. Her husband was out of town on a business trip, and her ninth-grade son was feeling depressed because he had been ignored by his basketball coach all season.

There are simply some days when you have to wonder why you do what you do!

*   *   *

Do the things that happened to Toni sound familiar? Perhaps you have been lucky enough not to have a single day quite as bad as the one described above. Or maybe the day that Toni just experienced was actually an easy day on your calendar. The point is that all principals, regardless of experience, level of school, size of school, type of school district, or any other variable that might be introduced, have very difficult, important, and demanding jobs. And the fact is that the job will likely become even more demanding, critical, and stressful in the future. As more states and school districts race toward the adoption of decentralized forms of educational governance and administration, the spotlight will be directed even more intensely on the principal's role in providing effective leadership. This fact must be recognized along with the other types of demands, expectations, and pressures that are placed on educators in general, and the principal in particular. Who could possibly imagine that elementary school principals (and principals in general) would someday be involved with disarming students who show up in schools carrying loaded pistols? And what about the need to deal effectively with youngsters who walk into school each day from homes where parents are child abusers, drug dealers, or other forms of felons and sociopaths? What do principals do when students arrive at their schools after spending the night sleeping on floors or in bathtubs while listening to the sound of gunshots in their neighborhoods?

We will end our listing of problems faced by modern principals at this point. For one thing, we're concerned that if we continue to list all of the problems, you will begin to question your decision about becoming a principal in the first place. Let us say, quite simply, that the benefits of being a principal will likely far outweigh the problems and frustrations in the long run. Nevertheless, it is critical, both for immediate success and for long-term survival, that you find some strategies to make certain that when the "alligators are nipping at your ankles," you don't get swallowed up. Even Toni was able to come back and face another day!

In this chapter, we offer a few strategies that have been identified by quite a few very successful (and surviving) school principals who have learned how to cope with the numerous frustrations and pressures they experience on the job. You may have already adopted some of these suggestions on your own, and in that case, you may be well beyond the advice we offer here. Or you might be in that unfortunate state where the problems and crises have been coming along so rapidly in your life that you haven't had much time to look up from your desk and find any useful survival strategies. In that case, this chapter could be extremely important.

Strategy #1: Find a Mentor

We truly believe that the single most powerful thing that a beginning principal (and even experienced principals) can do to enhance personal survival and effectiveness is to find at least one other experienced educational leader who can be available to share expertise related to doing the job more effectively and, perhaps even more important, help you understand yourself and your personal transition into the principalship more completely. A mentor can also help significantly with the complex task of becoming effectively socialized both into the overall profession of the principalship and also into the norms, culture, and practices of the district in which you find your first job.

Do you already have at least one mentor who is helping you during this initial introduction to the principalship? (If so, who is it, and what are some of the characteristics you have found in that person that make him or her particularly valuable to you as a mentor?)

Our research on administrative mentors over several years has found the following characteristics as related to individuals frequently identified as effective mentors to aspiring and beginning school principals. (Compare these qualities with the ones in the list that you have prepared above.)

1. Mentors are experienced administrators who are regarded by peers and others as effective.

2. Mentors demonstrate qualities of effective leaders, such as:
   - Good communication skills
   - Intelligence
   - Clear vision of what could be
   - Positive interpersonal skills and sensitivity

3. Mentors ask the right questions; they do not simply provide all the right answers.

4. Mentors accept others' ways of doing things; they do not want everyone else to do it their way.

5. Mentors desire other people to go beyond their present levels of performance.

6. Mentors model principles of continuous learning and reflection.

7. Mentors exhibit awareness of political and social realities of life in at least one school system.

By the way, you may have noticed the absence of some other characteristics that a lot of people have often assumed to be desirable in mentors. For example, many people assume that the most effective mentors are those with many years of experience as principals, as if survival on the job automatically results in wisdom and insight. Clearly, such experience is not always tied to effectiveness as a mentor. There are some individuals who have spent 20 years as principals, but unfortunately, they have done the same things for 20 years in a row! Consequently, they haven't grown, and they haven't learned from their own past experience. What are you likely to gain from working with people like this?

There is also an assumption that men must mentor men and that women can only mentor women. Although we have found that people often express a desire to have same-gender mentoring relationships (and for some reason, these are frequently easier to carry out), there is no research evidence that shows conclusively that men cannot be effective mentors to women (or vice versa). We believe that this is a comforting finding, particularly in the world of high school administration where relatively few experienced women principals can be found to mentor beginning female colleagues.

There is also an incorrect assumption that only older individuals can serve effectively as mentors to younger administrators. Perhaps this image comes from the traditional view that the only thing that a mentor does is to fill up the protege with a lot of "tricks of the trade" and lessons from the past. We believe that this is a very limited view of mentoring, and one that has the potential of being more harmful than helpful to your career. The reason is that in many cases, new principals have been hired precisely because there is a desire to "get some new blood" into the school system. There has been too long a history of doing the same things in the same ways. Mentors who see themselves only as people to help you do your job in an easier way may be inadvertently limiting your potential future success by telling you "how we've always done it around here."

Now that you have considered these additional issues regarding effective mentoring relationships, who are some individuals that you might identify as potentially effective mentors for you as a beginning principal? (These may or may not be the same people you thought of at the beginning of this chapter.)

_____

_____

_____

_____

Strategy #2: Develop Networks

Another strategy to help you survive the first few years in the principalship is to develop networks with other administrators. These can take several forms. For example, if you are one of several rookie principals in a district, county, or some other identifiable region, you may wish to get in contact with these other inexperienced administrators to form some kind of contract for mutual support. You may wish to agree to get together once a month for a social gathering during which you can share some of your "war stories" (or even "horror stories") about your life as a beginner. You will be surprised to learn that many of the "mistakes" that you believe that you have made are ones made by a good many of your beginning colleagues (and more experienced colleagues as well).

Do you know of any other beginning principals in your area with whom you might be able to form a mutual support network?

_____

_____

_____

_____

Networks have also been formed among women principals. Only a few years ago, this was a rarity. Now, women administrator leagues and networks have appeared all over the country, generally based on the assumption that because school administration has traditionally been a "man's game," it is critical to develop mutually supportive arrangements among those who want a share of the game. The same logic has been followed in the establishment of networks for representatives of ethnic and racial minority groups serving as school leaders.

We believe that the formation of networks is an important form of potential support that may assist you in the earliest stages of your career, with an important exception. We have seen some instances where the primary goal of a network apparently has been only to maintain itself, not necessarily to provide support to individual participants. It is likely that as one matures in a professional role, it will be less important to maintain membership in a mutual support arrangement, whether that arrangement is classified as mentoring or networking. In those cases, it is important that you feel free to determine your own continuing membership. A relationship of any kind is no longer healthy when participants feel as if they are forced to continue to stay involved.

Strategy #3: Participate in Professional Associations

As you begin a new career, you will receive invitations for membership in related professional organizations that provide opportunities for you to stay abreast of current education issues and to become politically involved. Although these organizations do require some dedication of your time and financial resources, we strongly recommend that you consider membership as a commitment to the improvement of not only your profession but also your own career.

Whether it is the National Association of Elementary School Principals (NAESP), the National Association of Secondary School Principals (NASSP), or the state and local affiliates of these nationwide organizations, belonging to an appropriate professional association has some clear and obvious benefits. For example, you will receive publications such as the *NASSP Bulletin* or the NAESP *Principal* magazine several times each year. These and the many other fine newsletters and reports provided by the associations will help you to remain in contact with important research, trends, and issues that face principals all over the nation. Most state affiliates also offer periodic publications to keep you informed regarding matters of interest to you and your colleagues on a more localized basis. Membership in professional associations also usually provides you with some form of professional liability insurance coverage that may help to keep you from financial damage if you happen to become involved in issues that may have legal consequences for you. Both NAESP and NASSP and their state affiliates also offer legal services "hotlines" to help you get feedback from lawyers and experienced administrators as you go about your daily work. Finally, membership in professional associations allows you to attend workshops, seminars, conferences, and conventions that help you maintain important social and professional contact with other principals across your state and around the nation.

Perhaps the single most important value to be gained from membership in relevant professional associations, however, has little to do with publications, legal services, liability insurance, or attendance at conventions. Simply stated, when you become involved in a national or state association of professional administrators, you develop a sense of belonging and involvement with your profession. By reading publications of your associations, attending meetings, and serving on committees, task forces, or other kinds of activities, you have a chance to hear or read about the world of administration through the eyes of other colleagues in other settings. Often, the job of principal feels like a lonely one because it seems that the problems and issues that you encounter are of such magnitude that no one else has ever faced these concerns. Working with colleagues from other school systems (and from other states on occasion) is a quick way to establish that you are not alone. Others are walking in your shoes.

Professional association memberships cost money, and that is a resource most principals do not have as a surplus, particularly in the first few years of their careers. Often, your first principalship comes soon after you have completed (and paid for) graduate studies at a university. You may have also recently had to pay to relocate to a new community. In some cases, new principals report pay cuts from what they were earning as classroom teachers. Nevertheless, membership in appropriate state, local, or national associations is a worthwhile investment that can assist you in your daily life as a professional administrator.

Strategy #4: Maintain Personal and Family Support

The fourth and final form of support that we recommend may be the most obvious, but it is often overlooked as people embark upon new careers. Often, the most powerful way to help newcomers to a field is found in one's natural, immediate environment. As you begin your career as an administrator, it is likely that your world will be filled with so many new responsibilities, people, and activities that you will become overwhelmed with many competing demands and interests. Suddenly, things and events that were important to you only a few months ago seem distant and less important as you work hard to develop a new professional identity and self-image. Although that is understandable, we suggest that it is critical to keep a personal focus on what is truly important in your life. Demands of a professional nature are important; the roots and foundation in your personal and family life are even more important and will be with you well beyond your career as a principal of a school.

Our first recommendation, then, is to make certain that, whenever possible, you do whatever is needed and reasonable to retain some sense of normality in your personal life. Do not ignore family and friends. If you are a high school principal with night duties during the basketball season, do not forget your son's piano recital or your daughter's basketball tournament. Remember that the annual trek to the seashore was a big part of your life when you were a fourth-grade teacher; it is still important now that you are an elementary school principal. Don't forget to return phone calls to personal friends who knew you back in the "old days," before you were such an important person. In short, keep your compass and perspective; don't forget what is really important to you. And remember that you can be a very effective and successful school leader even if you take a night off to do nothing more critical than watch a sappy old movie on the VCR.

The second recommendation that we make in this regard is related to your need to maintain your health. We remind you that critically ill principals are not very effective. Do not neglect matters of health, personal fitness, and well-being. This is important with respect to matters of physical well-being, and also emotional, intellectual, and even spiritual health. Go to the doctor when you are sick and for regular examinations, exercise, eat right (and don't fall into the "principal-as-martyr" syndrome that seemingly rewards people for never eating lunch, skipping breakfast, and drinking coffee all day), and take care of your body. Get out of your office, forget about your work once in a while, read a trashy novel, attend a movie or concert, or do any of a thousand things that will remind you of your need to get out of your role as an educational administrator on occasion. (This reminder may be a difficult one for you. Educators are notorious for their tendency to "eat, drink, and sleep" schools and talk shop all the time.) With regard to intellectual well-being, do something that challenges your mental capacity. We know school principals who regularly take university courses or participate in study groups that have nothing to do with the field of education as a way to keep their minds sharp; they enroll in language courses or other programs that seemingly have nothing to do with schools as a way to keep contact with their spiritual core. And with regard to spiritual well-being, if you have always been involved with church-related activities throughout your life, is there any reason to stop this involvement simply because you have the title of "principal" on your door?

We don't wish to sound as if we are prescribing all of the things that you might do to ensure that you maintain a balance among all of your priorities as a beginning school principal. We do not wish to suggest that your only route to happiness and success will be to maintain a perfect family life. After all, we realize there are times when principals have situations in their personal lives during which traditional patterns of home and happiness might be interrupted or changed. And those situations may have nothing to do with their effectiveness as a principal or their personal well-being. We also know there are times when it will be impossible to get to the gym, play a round of golf, or attend an opera, even though we just preached that these activities might be worthwhile. The critical message here is that it is not only a good idea but in some ways a critical responsibility for principals to think of their own personal needs above other issues.

Developing a Plan of Action

We conclude this chapter and this book by asking you to plan a systematic way of putting into effect many of the support mechanisms we have identified. Again, we are not suggesting that it is absolutely necessary for you to adopt all four strategies. However, we believe that it is important to select some clear ways in which you might reasonably expect to enjoy greater success in your job. We also believe that by taking time here to write out some of the sources of support you may find for yourself, you will become committed to these various approaches and activities.

Strategy #1: Find a Mentor

Who are some individuals who could serve in a mentoring capacity to you as you move into the principalship?

_____

_____

_____

_____

What are some of the specific concerns associated with your work as a principal that you believe might be addressed by a mentoring relationship?

_____

_____

_____

_____

Strategy #2: Develop Networks

Do you currently have any networks developed with other school principals?

_____

_____

_____

_____

In what specific ways might your network assist you in dealing with concerns and issues you face as a beginning principal?

_____

_____

_____

_____

Strategy #3: Participate in Professional Associations

Do you currently belong to any state, local, or national associations for school administrators? Which one(s)?

_____

_____

_____

_____

What are some of the activities of your association in which you participate? What personal or professional goals do you hope to achieve through these forms of participation?

_____

_____

_____

_____

Strategy #4: Maintain Personal and Family Support

List some of the ways in which you intend to spend more time with your family, engage in leisure activities, or simply "take care of yourself" during the next several months.

_____

_____

_____

_____

What are some of the personal and professional benefits that you hope to achieve?

_____

_____

_____

_____

Suggested Readings

In addition to suggestions for networks, mentors, and joining professional associations, other resources exist that may be of considerable help to you in your first years as a principal. Quite a few books are currently available to provide you with additional information about many of the things faced each day by school principals—whether new to the job or with a lot of experience.

A Framework for Understanding the Principalship

Barth, R. S. (1990). *Improving schools from within.* San Francisco: Jossey-Bass.

Bolman, L. G., & Deal, T. E. (1993). *The path to school leadership: A portable mentor.* Thousand Oaks, CA: Corwin.

Leithwood, K., Begley, P. T., & Cousins, J. B. (1995). *Developing expert leadership for future schools.* Washington, DC: Falmer.

Robbins, P., & Alvy, H. (1995). *The principal's companion: Strategies and hints to make the job easier.* Thousand Oaks, CA: Corwin.

Starratt, R. J. (1995). *Leaders with vision.* Thousand Oaks, CA: Corwin.

Reviewing Personal Values

Braham, B. (1994). *Finding your purpose: A guide to personal fulfillment.* Los Altos, CA: Crisp.

Chapman, E. N. (1991). *Career discovery program.* Los Altos, CA: Crisp.

Fritz, R. (1991). *Think like a manager.* Shawnee Mission, KS: National Seminar Publications.

Goman, C. K. (1991). *Managing for commitment.* Los Altos, CA: Crisp.

Heckman, P. E. (1996). *The courage to change.* Thousand Oaks, CA: Corwin.

Hunt, D. E. (1987). *Beginning with ourselves.* Cambridge, MA: Brookline Books.

Scott, C., Jaffe, D., & Tobe, G. R. (1993). *Organizational vision, values, and mission.* Los Altos, CA: Crisp.

Yockstick, M., & Jorstad, K. (1991). *Values and vision.* Boulder, CO: Marlin Associates International.

Being a "Boss"

Belker, L. B. (1993). *The first-time manager* (3rd ed.). New York: American Management Association.

Carr, C. (1989). *New manager's survival manual.* New York: John Wiley & Sons.

Hartzell, G. N., Williams, R., & Nelson, K. T. (1995). *New voices in the field.* Thousand Oaks, CA: Corwin.

A Personal Leadership Checkup

Goldring, E. B., & Rallis, S. F. (1993). *Principals of dynamic schools.* Thousand Oaks, CA: Corwin.

Gupton, S. L., & Slick, G. A. (1996). *Highly successful women administrators.* Thousand Oaks, CA: Corwin.

Sagor, R., & Barnett, B. G. (1994). *The TQE principal: A transformed leader.* Thousand Oaks, CA: Corwin.

Wallace, R. (1995). *From vision to practice: The art of educational leadership.* Thousand Oaks, CA: Corwin.

Technical and Managerial Skills

Burleson, C. W. (1990). *Effective meetings: The complete guide.* New York: John Wiley & Sons.

Haynes, M. E. (1988). *Effective meeting skills: A practical guide for more productive meetings.* Los Altos, CA: Crisp.

Hicks, A. T. (1996). *Speak softly & carry your own gym key: A female high school principal's guide to survival.* Thousand Oaks, CA: Corwin.

Katz, N. H., & Lawyer, J. W. (1991). *Communication and conflict resolution skills.* Dubuque, IA: Kendall Hunt.

National Association of Elementary School Principals. (1994). *Best ideas from America's Blue Ribbon Schools, Volume I: What award-winning elementary and middle school principals do.* Thousand Oaks, CA: Corwin.

National Association of Elementary School Principals. (1995). *Best ideas from America's Blue Ribbon Schools, Volume II: What award-winning elementary and middle school principals do.* Thousand Oaks, CA: Corwin.

National Association of Elementary School Principals. (1995). *Practical ideas that work.* Alexandria, VA: Author.

Quick, T. L. (1991). *Training managers so they can really manage.* San Francisco: Jossey-Bass.

Williams, A. B. (1993). *More than 50 ways to build team consensus.* Palatine, IL: IRI/Skylight.

A Personal Timeline for Development

Johnson, D. W. (1993). *Reaching out: Interpersonal effectiveness and self-actualization.* Boston: Allyn & Bacon.

Others' Expectations

Hunsaker, P. L., & Alessandra, A. J. (1980). *The art of managing people.* New York: Touchstone.

Henderson, N., & Milstein, M. M. (1996). *Resiliency in schools.* Thousand Oaks, CA: Corwin.

Reading the Signs in a System

Anderson, G. L., Herr, K., & Nihlen, A. S. (1994). *Studying your own school.* Thousand Oaks, CA: Corwin.

Herman, J., & Winters, L. (1992). *Tracking your school's success.* Newbury Park, CA: Corwin.

Finding Resources

Daresh, J. C., & Playko, M. A. (1993). *Leaders helping leaders: A practical guide to administrative mentoring.* New York: Scholastic.

Raye-Johnson, V. (1990). *Effective networking: Proven techniques for career success.* Los Altos, CA: Crisp.

CORWIN
PRESS

The Corwin Press logo—a raven striding across an open book—represents the happy union of courage and learning. We are a professional-level publisher of books and journals for K-12 educators, and we are committed to creating and providing resources that embody these qualities. Corwin's motto is "Success for All Learners."